REG RUSSE
01803-5

TOUCHED BY FROST

TOUCHED BY FROST

JIMMY FROST
WITH LUCY JOHNSON

DEDICATION

This book is dedicated to my parents who have been true pillars throughout my career, to Nikki and my family for putting up with me through thick and thin, and to everyone who has supported me. *Jimmy Frost*

Sincere thanks to Rick Cowdery, Sports Editor of the *Western Morning News*; Jonathan Powell and Brough Scott, for their support and enthusiasm and for believing we could turn Jimmy's story into a good yarn; to all Jim's friends, for being such valuable sources of information; to my mum and dad and to all my friends, including Pau, Simon, Jeremy, Julie and Jacques for putting up with me. *Lucy Johnson*

Published in 2003 by Highdown
an imprint of Raceform Ltd
Compton, Newbury, Berkshire, RG20 6NL
Raceform Ltd is a wholly owned subsidiary of MGN Ltd

A catalogue record for this book is available from the British Library.

ISBN 1-904317-26-X

Designed by Sam Pentin
Printed by CPD

CONTENTS _____

FOREWORD

It is right that the Frost story should be told so far, as the curtain has come down on one chapter, his jockey career, and he is now into his next, training. This, I'm sure, will be another story in its own right.

I had admired 'Frosty', as we called him, for many years when he rode on the Westcountry racing circuit, and he entered my life big time in the late Eighties. He had his first ride for me on Lucky Vane at Exeter in 1986 and it was the beginning of something extra special. Not only was it the forerunner of a most successful racing partnership, but also the start of a very happy relationship with an extraordinary man who has become a very dear friend.

A horseman by birth and a real competitor by nature, his formative years, when he rode to hounds, took part in gymkhanas, show jumped (you name it he did it) made him the complete rider. Add to this years of race riding on all sorts of horses and on many different courses, from point-to-points in the depths of Cornwall to tracks like Cheltenham and Sandown, and you had the total racing package – a canny race rider who could ride any horse to achieve its best result. This is what we had the privilege to work with at Fyfield and my early schooling ground description of 'long legs, no brain' was soon proved incorrect!

Jimmy rode for us during a purple patch at Fyfield and names like Lucky Vane, Kildimo, Morley Street, Forest Sun and Little Polveir (to name but a few) conjure up many happy memories. Of all the horses, Morley Street was undoubtedly the star, and I always feel that neither he nor Jimmy got the recognition they deserved for going to America and winning the Breeders' Cup Chase two years running, firstly at Belmont Park and then at Fair Hill.

Behind every successful person is a back up team and they deserve special mention – Jim's parents Richard and Glynne for their continual support and encouragement; his wife Nikki for delivering him up to Fyfield sound, light and happy on a regular basis and then the next generation, his children Daniel, Hadden and Bryony. They represent the future and are already actively involved in the whole Frost way of life. To all of them 'Thank You and Good Luck'.

Toby Balding
Kimpton
2003

CHAPTER 1

You Little Beauty

The 8th of April 1989 . . . I will never forget that day.
The day when a brave little horse took on the world and
came home a hero. The 8th of April will always belong
to Little Polveir; a horse who was named after a salmon
pool on the River Dee but was a bit of a tiddler himself,
standing less than 16 hands high.

People have spent whole careers trying to get the big-
race results, but we did it. We won the Grand National.
It had all come together somewhat by chance. I
happened to be at Fyfield working for Toby Balding
and Ted Harvey, Little Polveir's owner, happened to
phone up – it was fate. We couldn't have planned it.

A few days before the National, I was in the car with
Toby, with whom I had a retainer, and he was talking
about the horses he intended to run at Aintree. After
Cheltenham, his star hurdler Morley Street had got a
big splinter in a leg going over a hurdle and initially it
looked like Aintree was off the calendar. But it had
healed really well and he was back on target. He was

my star ride and we were going for the Mumm Novices' Hurdle.

I had about four rides at the meeting, including General Chandos, who was to give me my first experience over the National fences in the John Hughes. It was almost as an afterthought that Toby informed me that Little Polveir was going to run in the Grand National.

"Brilliant!" I thought.

I had reached the age of 30 and suspected that any chance I had of ever riding in the Grand National, let alone winning it, had gone.

People were always asking me what I did for a living. "I ride horses," I'd say.

"What sort of horses?" they would ask.

"National Hunt horses," I'd reply.

"Oh really – you're a jump jockey then. Have you ever ridden in the Grand National?" they'd ask.

Every time I would have to say "no," and they would be thinking: "He's no good then."

So you can imagine my delight that at last I could say I'd ridden in the race, even if it meant we only got as far as the first fence.

*

The Aintree meeting starts on Thursday, so on Tuesday and Wednesday I went down to Fyfield to pop Little Polveir over a few fences. He did it so easily it was like painting by numbers despite the fact Seamus Mullins, Toby's amateur at the time, had informed me that only a few days earlier they had used him to give some young horses a lead over fences and he had refused to jump anything.

Toby was winding me up before the National. He was in one of his 'let's get at Jim' moods. I had ridden General Chandos, a difficult horse, in the John Hughes on the Thursday and been beaten. Beforehand, Steve Smith Eccles' verdict had been: "You're going down."

We didn't go down, but we did finish fourth to the favourite, Villierstown. I was pretty pleased because he always jumped to the right and Aintree is left-handed. I thought we had done well to get round. He also made some pretty hair-raising blunders at the first, second and 15th; all of which we had managed to survive.

But Toby was not happy. He said: "Frost, you'd better pull yourself together. You are never going to win any decent races riding like this."

I was being a little bit laid back. So, by adopting his forcing tactics, Toby was trying to get me more on the ball. He was pretty wound up anyway and to make matters worse, on the Friday before the National, he expected Farm Week to win the EBF Diamond Edge Challenge Trophy at Devon and Exeter. We were joint-favourites with Flying God at 9-2, even though he had 10st 12lbs and the seven-pound claimer Willie McFarland on board, and my horse had a double penalty, having won at Folkestone and Worcester, and 12st 5lbs to lump round.

Predictably, we were beaten some 25 lengths. That day I'd been taken off Romany King, after I could get no further than fourth in the EBF Novices' Hurdle Qualifier at Wincanton in March 1989 and then Richard Guest won the Haldon Moor Novices' Hurdle on him by a good margin. I was so annoyed because the horse had run out of petrol at the last at Wincanton, but all I could do was sit and watch Guesty take all the credit.

Lorna Vincent, who was riding under Rules at the time, wanted a lift to Aintree from Exeter so we got straight in the car, picking up another jockey friend Jamie Railton at Strensham services on the M5 on the way. Soon after we left Exeter, Toby was on the phone wanting a report on his horses. He found it hard to accept that Farm Week had been beaten and, not being totally inspired by my ride on General Chandos on the Thursday, he gave me a telling-off.

My confidence was really waning. Perhaps I wasn't any good? Perhaps he should get someone else to do this job and I should go home? I could say very little back as Lorna was sitting beside me and I have never been one to run from criticism. Toby threw every expletive in the book at me but, unless he was actually going to sack me, I'd keep going.

We arrived at Warrington, just outside Liverpool, where BTRB, Toby's racing club, had taken over rooms at a hotel. Jamie and Lorna dropped me off there and went on to Liverpool in my car. It was a good club with a lot of nice members. We had dinner but I had to ride at 10st the next day, so I had to sit and play with my food instead of eating it. I went to bed early, planning an early start in the sauna before Jamie picked me up at 9.30am, when I could get back behind the wheel of my car.

I was so busy chatting to Jamie and my mind was a million miles away from the road, that we jumped a red traffic light and, as luck would have it, a policeman pulled me over.

"What's your name?" he asked. I told him, and recognising it, he asked what I was riding in the Grand National and if we had a chance.

"Yeah, good each-way bet. Put a tenner on, but don't give me a ticket will you?" I asked. And he let me off.

By the time we arrived at the course at 10am, the atmosphere of Grand National day was beginning to build. Friends and relations were wishing us luck and the noticeboard in the weighing room was filled with telegrams. There were journalists and photographers everywhere.

After depositing my bag in the weighing room, I had a walk round the course on my own, planning my ride as I went. I still hadn't made my mind up where to go but I had some idea of where I wanted to be, having ridden General Chandos at Aintree.

I already knew Toby's instructions were going to be to hunt him round on the first circuit and ride a race on the second, so I decided to jump off on the inside down to Becher's the first time, track across and get back to the inside, because you definitely save a lot of time by doing that. However, the plan never came off and I ended up riding on instinct rather than pre-conceived ideas, which is the way I always ride best – just like I had ridden in point-to-points.

I couldn't have felt happier walking round. It felt as though the circumstances around which life revolves were gradually coming together for Little Polveir that day. He had a high wither and a bit of a dippy back but he was built like a battleship and he had a great big backside. He was a strong, old-fashioned type, pretty in his own way, and with a lovely front. Toby had bought him six weeks before the Grand National with an entry in the race. He'd been in training with John Edwards, but Colonel Ted Harvey bought him for his son David to ride in the Grand Military Cup at Sandown. He did the job very nicely and carried him around to finish fourth.

The horse didn't lack experience – he'd been over the National fences four times before, and I knew he jumped well. I studied the video and decided to do exactly as Tom Morgan had the year before, with one or two slight amendments. He'd been right up there in 1988 going over Valentine's the last time, but horse and rider had got their wires crossed at the take-off. Tom had gone "one, two, three, now!" and Little Pol said "no", so I reckoned that, in order to get on with the horse, you had to let him get in deep.

Before he fell, he was arguably going like the winner. "Do you know, Nikki? I reckon if we can get a clear round I've got a feeling we can get in the first three from the way he was going last year," I said to my wife.

But you have to be realistic. I'd never ridden in the race before, so if I got round in one piece, I'd have been delighted. I'd galloped him, Morley Street and the rest of the gang in the week leading up to the National and he felt fine, but there was nothing about him that really excited me. He didn't have a huge stride, he wasn't particularly fast; he was just a nice horse.

My biggest worry on National day was that I would get injured riding in the big one and wouldn't be able to ride Morley Street later in the day. But all those silly paranoid thoughts soon leave you once you're in the weighing room. I had another small sweat so that I could ride at 10st 3lbs.

*

Time flies pretty quickly in the build up to the race, and before you know it you are under the spotlight. You have butterflies in your stomach and you get psyched up because you are about to undertake a huge challenge. You have to be mentally sharp, so you close your mind to everything else and focus on what's ahead of you.

Toby had more or less left it up to me to decide how to run the race, but in the paddock, with Mr Harvey and all his family, he once again advised me to hunt Little Polveir around on the first circuit and then to ride a race on the second.

As we left the paddock and went out to parade, with his lass Fiona Hambleton at his head, we eventually assembled into our numbered order, number 21. We walked in front of the grandstand, deep in thought but nonetheless relaxed.

The parade went pretty quickly and the noise level was building. It sounded tremendous, with constant cheering. I daren't look into the grandstand; it was too awesome. Fiona slipped the lead rein and Little Polveir took the bit. I started to feel the job was now in my hands.

We cantered down to the first fence and then back to the start. The horses were starting to jostle each other, the atmosphere was becoming increasingly electric and Little Polveir was getting excited.

I'd had a dream the night before that my leathers had broken in the race so I couldn't get comfortable with the length. One hole felt too short, the other too long, and, amidst all the melee of the start, all I could think was I wish I had a hole in between the two. We took a turn, and then another. I didn't want to be at the back so

I kept at the front. Everything would be perfect, then we'd take another turn. And all the time, I was up and down in the saddle.

The starter Keith Brown called the 40-strong field in for a second time. He shouted: "Jockeys in a line, jockeys in a line. Wait, wait...Come on!"

I thought: "Get there quick because everything will be away." The next second, we were going like a cavalry charge down to the first fence.

There are horses all around you and all you have is elbowroom, but we had a great run across the Melling Road and down to the first fence. We were going a good gallop, Little Pol was focused and we jumped the first well.

I caught sight of Hettinger's colours, worn by Ray Goldstein and thought: "Oh shit." He was the one horse I told myself not to get behind. I wouldn't have tracked him round Plumpton, let alone Aintree.

I'd gone through every set of colours, I knew every horse in the race, and I was stuck behind the worst one. I moved to the right, to the middle of the track and immediately picked up Richard Dunwoody on West Tip – I'd gone from the worst to the best. We tracked him down to Becher's and the fences were coming up much quicker than anything I had experienced.

There are so many horses and you can't focus because you only have a small window in front of you. The drop on the fences is that bit more and you dwell in the air before you land. The rattle of the timber is immense.

Little Pol jumped out over Becher's and pecked on landing, but there were no fallers in front of me and after two or three strides we had got away with it. The field got tight towards the next fence as we all moved to the inside and the horses were side by side, almost lifting you into the air.

But Little Pol was the ultimate professional and kept going. It was his fourth Grand National and he knew more than I did. At the Canal Turn, he jumped left so quickly that I nearly came out the side door to the right.

"Shit, I'll leave this to him," I thought and we galloped on down towards Valentine's. We were now in fourth on the inside, we jumped Valentine's, crossed the Melling Road and came back onto the course. We were really galloping, jumping a lot of fences, and Little Pol was going well.

Coming down to what would be the second-last with a circuit to run, Little Pol started to pull the reins out of my hands. Until that point he had been travelling very well with an easy rhythm.

"Come on, steady, fella," I said. Two loose horses came up on the inside and we were in tight to the wing. He started to get out of his rhythm and that was his first real mistake. We got in deep to what would have been the last and I actually let go with one hand. The loose horses disappeared out of the way and he settled down into a rhythm again as we headed towards the Chair. He'd pulled himself to the front and was really running.

Three of us came to the Chair together and I have never concentrated on anything so much in my life. It was like looking through binoculars that were slightly out of focus. The fence comes towards you and suddenly there is a crystal clear picture. I'm on five strides one . . . two . . . three . . . four . . . five. We are just in front of the board and he sailed over as if it was an ordinary open ditch.

We'd got the Chair out of the way and jumped the water nicely. West Tip was up there on my right-hand side and we were knee to knee, with me on the inside.

"How's yours?" I asked Richard.

"Yep, got round the first circuit now we've got to go and do it all again. Once is enough isn't it?" he replied.

From that point we were on our own. Little Pol had taken it up and I wasn't doing anything. He had rhythm and balance and was travelling so well I felt we were only in third gear.

We hit the open ditch. "Shit," I thought, but he was so clever he bounced over and got away with it. That was our only near-disaster. I had tried to get him to stand off but he needed a little short one and got so close he actually put a front foot on the rail of the ditch. Another inch or two and we'd have been buried at the bottom, but somehow he paddled the fence and got himself out of trouble.

We soared over Becher's second time with a clear lead and were waved wide. I just caught a glimpse of Brown Trix lying dead on the outside.

"Good boy, Pol. You're doing well, chap," I talked to him all the way round. He jumped Foinavon, where in 1967 a horse with that name avoided a pile-up at the 23rd obstacle to record a 100-1 shock victory. We came to the Canal very tight to the inside and Richard shouted, "Give me a bit of room." And we showjumped it on the turn.

We landed tight to the inside, he made an excellent turn and we set off down the far side for a second time.

The fences were looking a lot lower and I started to kick Little Pol on a bit to get some energy from him. Now we were racing.

"Rhythm, concentrate, rhythm, keep him going," I thought and he was so responsive that I dropped my left hand a bit and he turned to the right immediately. He was still very responsive – a tired horse won't do that.

"Christ, I've got a bit of horse left," I thought.

We crossed the Melling Road again and I thought, "When Daniel goes to school, he can tell everyone that when his dad rode in the National he led the field back onto the racecourse proper."

We came round the rail and there were some lager louts jumping about on the track. "Oh shit," I thought, "We'd better go round them, which is going to spoil it." We were on the bend leading with the right leg and, if I'd pulled him out to go round them, it would have broken his rhythm, so I thought I'll just keep my line and if they don't get out of the way I'll hit them. If they stay there, unlucky.

They moved, thank goodness, because, with hindsight, if I had run into them, they would probably have brought me down. Their antics later prompted a police inquiry.

You lose the running rail for a while at this point, and the loose horse Smart Tar had come around on my outside. It looked like he was going to take me out with him onto the Mildmay course, so I picked Little Pol up a half-stride, leant against Smart Tar and pushed him back onto the National track. We were lucky.

We jumped the second-last, but I didn't have a lot of horse under me. I could hear horses behind me. We jumped the last and I picked up my stick and asked for an effort up the run-in. Horses were coming at me, but we weren't really going. It felt like we were treading water and were probably going to drown. He was feeling heavy and was slowing down. "We're going to get caught, Pol, come on," I said. It was a feeling of desperation as I tried to regenerate some energy into his tired muscles.

He wasn't happy when I gave him a couple of slaps with the whip so I used my hands and heels and the energy button came on. Smart Tar had joined us and we were locked together. Little Pol started to lengthen his stride 100 yards before the line. My God, that finishing straight is long and the crowd is unbelievable. I thought 26,000 people had made some noise when we won at Kempton Park on Boxing Day, but 75,000 at Aintree is something else.

I can see now that we looked like getting swallowed up at the last – there were still so many fancied horses right there. But I wasn't looking round, I daren't. I might have panicked and unbalanced him.

The loose horse (Smart Tar) helped because basically Little Polveir was getting tired and he'd been in front for so long. His concentration was waning and Smart Tar helped him find his strength. I just kept riding for all I was worth, and he just kept going too. I couldn't believe what was happening now.

"They won't get me now, they're not going to get me." I said to myself.

We passed the post seven lengths clear of the fast finishing West Tip, with The Thinker third and Lastofthebrownies fourth. Little Polveir had done it all himself and looked after me like I was a baby. He did it beautifully.

*

Brendan Powell was the first to congratulate me. Stearsby had refused at the tenth but Brendan had got back on and was waiting near the finish as we pulled up. Little Pol's lass Fiona, who hadn't even had a bet on him because she was too superstitious, came running out with tears down her face, but it still didn't sink in that we had won.

It's almost like you are someone else, because there is so much to take in. I'd talked about the Grand National since I was six years old and the feelings are unimaginable. It's as if you are on the current of a strong river, out of control, and you just ride the waves and keep going. Other races have been a tremendous achievement, like the Breeders' Cup Chase and the Champion Hurdle, but there is only one National. Even now, I don't believe I have won it. It changes your life and you are put on a pedestal. You can't hide that because it's history.

Coming back into the winner's enclosure was a special moment. Everyone wants to congratulate you but there are too many people to take in; the lads you ride with day in and day out, John Buckingham the valet and many others.

Toby's first words to me were: "Good jockey, long legs and no brain." He was always quick to ensure his jockeys did not start to believe their own headlines, but he was full of praise after that race and he told the press: "Jimmy is as good a horseman as you'll see on the circuit, and they looked after each other out there.

"I've always maintained the National is a race for hunting folk, and Jimmy is a long-legged lad who gives a horse a chance."

You are rushed off here and there. I had to meet the Duchess of York and then came the presentation. But I also had to ride Morley Street in the next race. That was the thing about the National. If I'd got injured, I couldn't ride him. He flew round. Beech Road had won earlier in the day so it was Toby's day.

Toby had already won the National 20 years earlier with Highland Wedding, but he was still modest about his achievements. He said: "John Edwards has really trained this horse, I've just done nothing wrong for the past six weeks!"

But, ironically, before the race John Edwards had still held the trump card in the shape of the hugely fancied Dixton House. As it was, neither of Mr Edwards' contenders had managed to get round. Dixton House had fallen when right up with the leaders at Becher's on the first circuit, while Bob Tisdall disgraced himself by giving all the others a furlong start and then refusing at the second.

The race had been run at a slog and only the 1972 winner Well To Do and Ben Nevis, who won in 1980, had recorded a time slower than our 10 minutes 6.9 seconds. I had put up 3lbs overweight and Little Pol had actually carried 10lbs more than Christopher Mordaunt had allotted him. He was the first 12-year-old to win since Ben Nevis.

He was a grand old lad and he took me to the highest peak as a jockey. He never recaptured that form and he was never placed again because Aintree excited him and brought out his spark. I rode him at Cheltenham in the four-miler but, to him, it was like playing Premier League football and then turning out for a Sunday league team. I will always be grateful to him. He died after suffering a bout of colic on 22 February 1999, aged 22.

*

My family and I were all so naive about winning the National. Nikki had taken a bottle of champagne in case I got round but I was too tired to really appreciate the magnitude of the day. My parents have never shown much emotion. "That was good wasn't it?" was their summing up of the race. But I knew they were very proud of me, although there was no opening of a champagne bottle or suggestion that we might celebrate. They were happy to stay in the background and let me take all the glory.

As soon as I came out of the changing room people swamped me. It took me half an hour to get to my car. Jamie Railton was waiting for me and we drove back to the hotel at Warrington where BTRB members met me. I signed some autographs and shared a drink and then we went back to Strensham, where Jamie picked up his car.

It normally takes two hours to get home from Strensham. I did it in one hour and 35 minutes – who says diesel cars are slow? Family and close friends were waiting for me at the Dartmoor Hotel at Ashburton. Next day I had to go back to Fyfield and it was then that it all started to sink in as my life was thrown into turmoil. The media attention is extraordinary. I was filmed doing every conceivable thing bar the obvious, and for a few weeks, mine and Nikki's lives belonged to the press. Journalists were everywhere.

It was wonderful parading Morley Street, Beech Road and Little Polveir – I felt so proud for those horses. Toby and Caro soaked up the occasion. They were naturals at it.

A career in racing always has you on the edge but that week the attention was so intense and ultimately draining that, by the time the Scottish National came round a week later, I had no trouble doing 10st on Glenside Jerry, when my normal racing weight was 10st 3lbs.

However, despite the adulation, winning the National wasn't a licence to print money and I earned exactly £6,656, which was ten per cent of the prize money, and £56 for riding the horse. Compare that to winning the British Open or Wimbledon and it is peanuts. That summer, I was back on Paignton beach giving donkey rides and tending my 70 head of cattle.

CHAPTER 2

The Best Possible Beginning

Winning the Grand National in 1989 was the realisation of a dream born 17 years earlier. A dream that emerged on a snowy day in Cornwall when, as a 13-year-old, I won my first ever point-to-point.

Each man is said to be an architect of his own success but mine has been a chain of lucky coincidences which led to that momentous win because when I was nothing more than a twinkle in my father's eye, I played no part in the decision of two families called Middlemass and Frost to come to Devon.

My mum, Glynne, was brought up in London but came to Lustleigh in Devon with her mother and brother Stuart when the Second World War broke out. Grandfather had been among the first Allied soldiers into the Nazi concentration camp at Belsen in Germany. He only talked about this traumatic experience once, telling me he had seen starving Jews trying to catch rats to eat them. His experiences during the war had a profound effect on him, and by the time mum married dad when she was 20, granddad was already an alcoholic. He was a wonderful person and would dry up from time to time, when he would take me around to shows, and for several years he worked for the Coakers at Sherberton. However, he could never shake off his memories of the war.

The Middlemasses stayed in Devon and bought a house called Little Greendown at Holne, on Dartmoor. Grandfather Frost, a wealthy London businessman, retired from his job in the City and bought a farm at Holne with the idea that my father Richard, who had trained as a farrier at Warehams Forge in Epsom, would run it.

Mum spent all her time helping dad on the farm and eventually they fell in love. Sadly, grandfather Frost died a short time after he came to Devon. Grandma Frost didn't like mum, so she would have nothing to do with my dad and sold the farm. She retired to a bungalow on Jersey, which left mum and dad with nowhere to live. They rented some stables at the back of Holne Chase; dad started a farriery round and mum started doing horses.

Fortunately, one of dad's uncles, who was an officer in the Navy, had left him £5,000 in his will when he passed away. Hawson Court Cottage, which is located just a couple of miles away from Dartmoor, came up for sale and mum and dad bought it and moved in. I've been there ever since.

Hawson was a wonderful place to grow up, surrounded by woodland and with lovely views. There are so many places to hack out horses and ponies that even the most jaded or obstinate animal can be sweetened up. There are about 12 acres, and horses thrive in the pastures.

*

As well as running a trekking centre and buying and selling horses and ponies, my parents used to hire out hunters, so to all intents and purposes I was brought up on the back of a pony. The local packs were either the Dartmoor or the Spooners and West Dartmoor, whose master was Major Michael Howard.

My first appearance in the hunting field was on Brown Eyes one cold November day on Dartmoor. I was two years old, and I must have looked like a pea on a drum sat on my pony with dad clutching hold of the end of a lead rein. We kept up with the hounds for a couple of hours and eventually lost them at the back of Two Bridges Hotel.

"Come on son, time for us to go home," said dad, who had done well to keep up for so long.

"I don't want to go home yet!" I wailed. And for fear of denting my early enthusiasm for hunting, dad trudged on, taking a tributary of the River Dart in his stride. He was wet to his waist but kept going until I fell asleep on Brown Eyes. Only when I was dozing was he safe to turn back without any repercussions from a wilful small child. Dad needn't have worried. My introduction had me hooked and from the early days I became a hunting fanatic.

Hunting over Dartmoor, across bogs, over the ditches and through the streams, taught me to stick on. It's wild terrain and, for fear of being lost in a bog, you have to keep up with the pace, no matter what you are riding. I soon learnt that, if hounds were on a line, you kicked on; getting stuck out on the middle of the moor on your own is a scary proposition. Out there, often miles away from the nearest road, you sometimes feel as if it is a question of survival. You stay hard on the heels of the horse in front but just far enough back to pull up, should it fall into a bog. Those moors taught me how to ride.

From an early age, my job was to hold the hunters if the riders wanted to get off and have a pee. I was also called upon to open all the gates. However, I very nearly gave up altogether when I realised how much it hurt when you fell off.

When I was eight, I started to ride out the odd racehorse mum and dad had, including a lovely big old fellow who was patent safety. Not this day, however. We got left behind and he put in a huge buck and as the ground came up to meet me, I thought: "That's it. I'm not riding again."

It really put me off, so mum bought me a little pony called Marmaduke. I rode him around and soon insisted that she let me go hunting again. He was a Dartmoor-cross-Shetland and a big woolly bear, so mum clipped him out and off I went to a meet on the moor.

Mrs Howard, the master's wife, came looming up ahead of me on her big, smart hunter and as I looked up at her, we collided in a small gap. She tripped over my pony and went splat while I kicked like hell, leaving her coughing and spluttering and cursing me.

Eventually, after another incident in a ploughed field when Marmaduke ran out of petrol, I realised it was time I got a bigger pony. He would run as fast as his little legs could carry him but that was never quite fast enough. There was a man who used to hunt regularly. I didn't know who he was, but I always thought he looked well matched by his big, fat cob as he barged, puffed and panted his way round. He was the type of person who always managed to leave his manners at home every time he went hunting.

The man shouted: "Get out of my way. If I catch you I'm going to hit you with my hunting whip." I didn't stay long enough to find out whether he was serious. Marmaduke and I quickly disappeared over the horizon, me with my legs flapping against the saddle 19 to the dozen. Marmaduke had to go.

*

Mum and dad sat me on a number of different ponies but the first real hunting pony I could call my own was Spotty, and he became a major part of my life. He was the type of animal you would never find for looking. Standing about 12.2hh, he was a brilliant hunter, fantastic at gymkhanas and jumping and, to cap it all, he had loads of little white spots, a grey mane and a black tail, which meant that I was the centre of attention wherever we went, and that is something I have never minded.

Mum had bought Spotty for me at Sherberton pony sales, which was held every year near Princetown on Dartmoor. All the local farming community would gather each summer for a chinwag, along with serious buyers who were more intent on viewing the ponies. And each year, I'd go up to the Coakers' farm and jump on the ponies in the ring to show them off.

Spotty came up for sale and made 67 guineas. I had really taken to him as soon as he came into the ring. He stood out from the rest of the ponies, although I never thought for a minute I would be lucky enough to own him. But I remember the auctioneer banging the hammer down and saying "Frost." I was just seven years old and so pleased that I had my own flashy little pony coming back home with me to Hawson Court.

I couldn't ride one side of him at first. He was so wilful that Sally King, who later married my uncle Stuart Middlemass, rode him for me until eventually he realised that two wilful thinkers together could make a good team. That winter, I practised gymkhana games on him in the barn every night when I got home from school, and by the following summer we were like little professionals. He became a very good friend to me and looked after me for many years.

We had an amazing rapport and he was always one step ahead of the other ponies just as I was of their riders. Together we won more than 2,000 rosettes in gymkhanas. We also represented the Dartmoor Pony Club at the All England Championships as individuals in Hampshire. It was quite a big thing winning that.

Of course, I had plenty of other ponies, but Spotty was special. He loved his gymkhanas as much as I did and we had a mutual trust in each other. Onlookers may have got the impression that I was flat out and out of control in gymkhana races, which were often held in fields as hard as concrete in the height of summer, but Spotty would always pull up at the last possible moment and turn on a sixpence. Every weekend Spotty and I would hunt and some of my experiences in the hunting field make me shudder now, but as a kid you just pick yourself up again and ride on.

For years, Rodney Woodcock was the whipper-in with the Spooners and he'd always stay on the fringes, picking up loose hounds. We were at Dunnabridge, crossing from the West Dart to Sherberton New Takes. Rodney started crossing and his horse fell and Rodney fell off. His wife, who was following, also fell in. I thought: "I'm not brave enough for this," and set off for another crossing at Sandy Pool, so I was all on my own. The river was in flood but if you know the crossing, you can make it. You have to follow the bank and then cross, rather than go straight out, because there is a ledge. Of course I didn't know this and under we went. I could see bubbles and kept saying: "Come up Spotty, come up."

He was under the river swimming as hard as he could and somehow he got me across to the other side. I was soaking wet from the shoulders down, so I abandoned hunting and went to find Diana Coaker at Sherberton, who put my pony in a stable and dried me off by the Aga.

The Coakers are the oldest tenants of the Duchy of Cornwall and Diana's ponies are famous all over Europe. From an early age, I loved spending time with her. She was a great point-to-point rider over the banks and, if she had been a boy, I'm sure she would have ridden in the Grand National.

When I was on Spotty, I didn't think about drowning myself, but I was scared for the pony. Thankfully he was ok, and he was so brave that the next time I rode him, he went straight into a stream again at the back of the Clay Pits at Cornwood. And, as before, he struggled out again.

A few years later, when I was 11, hounds met at Walkhampton and we ended up in Burrator woods. It was three o'clock in mid-December and the light was starting to fade. Hounds had hunted hard all day and we hadn't stopped for miles. I was desperate for a wee but felt a bit embarrassed despite never batting an eyelid when nature had called for all those people for whom I held horses. So I didn't tell anyone about my plight and disappeared up a track. After doing what I had to, I rode back to the track to discover everybody had gone.

I wasn't sure how to find the lorry, but I knew that if I went across the moor it would bring me to the Princetown road and I knew once I was there I would be able to find my way home. I decided to stick to the road and galloped along the verges. I didn't give a moment's thought to dad, his four hunters and everyone else who was out on the moor wondering where I had vanished. It's 14 miles home and I did it in one and a quarter hours.

The search parties set out in earnest, scrutinising the bogs and wondering if I'd been sucked into one. Dad eventually found a house with a phone and broke the news to mum that her only son had been lost out on the moors.

"That's all right," she said. "He's sat here having a cup of tea." If dad had got hold of me at that moment, I think he would have killed me.

I could be an awkward so-and-so and, a couple of years later, when dad needed me to go hunting to keep an eye on the hirelings I refused. "Will you go if you can ride the mule?" he asked. Anything to be different, so I said yes.

She was about 15hh and was one of several mules a TV production company had hired from dad for the series *The Onedin Line*. She hunted well and would jump about three feet. I took her to Princetown where hounds were meeting and she caused havoc. Half the horses fell in love with her, the others were completely spooked and I had a great time. How I didn't get sent home, I will never know.

One poor chap had hired a hunter from George Cornish, who ran a riding school at Dousland, and probably only came out twice a year. His horse would not leave that mule alone. I told him to go through a gateway, wait there and allow me to set off home. Ten minutes later he was galloping after me.

"Why the hell did you have to bring that creature hunting?" he shouted. I couldn't blame him for getting so angry. His bi-annual pilgrimage to Dartmoor had ended in failure and he was also panicking because he was on a hireling, often an unknown quantity, and he didn't have a clue where he was. But there was nothing much I could do about it.

*

I learnt a lot about the countryside whilst I was growing up and I am still a tremendous supporter of hunting. My views today have probably changed, though, because I no longer think you can call it a sport. When I was younger, I didn't think twice about shooting a fox and leaving it half dead in the hedgerow – doubtless a healthy, fit animal that should have been spared to reproduce for the next generation.

If hunting goes, the countryside will be filled with people behaving like I used to; shooting every animal that comes across their path. Foxes have to be controlled and, aside from slaughter in an abattoir, hunting is the most humane method available. Marksmen draw no distinction between what they shoot – pregnant vixens, healthy dog foxes, as well as sick and old animals. There is nobody alive who can guarantee to shoot a fox dead every time in the wilds of the countryside.

Hunting naturally allows the strong healthy foxes to breed for the next year's generation and the chase sorts out the weak from the strong. It's natural culling. It is the fox's welfare that really bothers me. How many people are able to actually shoot a fox dead instantly? And if snares are used, how can they discriminate between the healthy or pregnant foxes and those that need culling?

CHAPTER 3

Advanced Beginner

For a Devon lad who spent the better part of his life haring around on ponies on the edge of Dartmoor, the glitz of Columbia Pictures was not something I could relate to, let alone knew existed. But when I was ten years old, the film industry landed on Dartmoor, and I was not only given a taste of life as an actor but also given a valid reason to miss school. David Rook, who had come to Sherberton as an evacuee during the war, had written the book *The White Colt,* which was to be turned into the film *Run Wild, Run Free,* starring Mark Lester.

They needed a special stunt rider and Diana Coaker, who had initially supplied the ponies, had told the producers about me.

"But he's got black hair," said Diana.

"Oh that won't do," said the producer. "His parents will never let him bleach it."

"These parents will," replied Diana.

I was duly summoned, jumped on a waiting pony,

galloped him up and down, jumped a stream, and was given the job as Mark Lester's double. My hair was bleached (I hopped around for four hours because it was so painful) and I looked a picture with dark brown eyebrows. But those moments of pain were worth it because I refused to go back to school until my blond hair had grown out.

The film was about a small boy called Philip who had a speech impediment and clammed up every time he tried to talk. He spent a lot of time on the moor and established a bond with a wild pony. John Mills played the part of an old moor man who kept the boy's relationship with the pony a secret.

Philip was riding the pony when a pack of hellhounds on the moor caused him to take fright. He came off and the pony disappeared. He was terribly upset, so the moor man tried to get him to focus on something else and gave him a kestrel called Lady. Philip took Lady out onto the moors on his own, allowed her to fly, and then returned home with the bird attached to her swivel and leash.

On his way back he saw a group of ponies and ran towards them. Lady was thrown violently, her wings were flapping and her beak was open. Eventually she lost her grip and went berserk and swung out of control. He had killed Lady. The pony came back again but ended up in a bog. A search party rescued the pony and Philip spoke again.

The filmmakers constructed an artificial bog on the moor with a concrete floor and post and rails to keep the pony in the centre. It was filled with green-dyed water and a raft was constructed for Philip to reach the pony. But when they showed the rushes, it looked so unrealistic that they decided to use a real bog. Diana's pony, which was a true moorland type, refused to go in, and Diana started to resist because she was concerned for his welfare.

They wouldn't use me to get the pony in because they said it was too dangerous, and summoned professional stuntmen from London. A man called Russell Forehead, who worked on *Lawrence of Arabia* and *The Charge of the Light Brigade,* brought three Palomino ponies to Dartmoor. The Palominos were kept in a large marquee, which was heated as they got so cold when the stuntmen attempted to get them to walk into the bog.

The stuntmen could not get the ponies in and fell off as soon as they hit the edge of the bog. The film's stars, who included Sylvia Sims and John Mills, would all have bets to see if they could get the ponies into the bog.

Russell suggested they use me, and I got them straight into the bog. As bogs go, it was beautiful – black in the middle but deceptively green and inviting on the edges. I hate bogs now. They frighten the life out of me.

For me, it was a fantastic holiday and I had five months off school and was getting paid to ride ponies. I did a lot of the work with Lady and all the riding on the pony. We had our own mobile homes, and we had a big blonde Australian chaperone who was supposed to teach us, but we had walkie-talkies and would disappear into the rocks on the moor. We ran terrible circles around the poor girl and she couldn't control us.

I received a lovely letter at the end, telling me I had done well and that, if I was interested in following up with a speaking part in another film, I should get in contact with them. But I was too young to realise what the film world was all about and, anyway, I had a one-track mind . . . ponies.

*

My winters were spent hunting and spinning around hunter trials, while the summers were for gymkhanas. As I became more adept on the ponies, we plundered the local shows, and even went as far as entering a mule in a donkey derby although, on our part, it was only a bit of fun.

In 1972, Chagford Show had come around again – a real country affair where all the locals turn out en masse to show off their stock and pick holes in those of their neighbours. We had entered Rupert, our mule, in the race and the judges were placed on the spot when an objection was placed. After conferring, they decided he was ineligible, although he had been fine to race the previous year.

"You can compete for fun but you are not allowed to win a prize," said one of the organisers.

But they needn't have worried – there was no chance of that. Rupert had the crowds roaring with laughter as he decked me three times, ran the reverse way around the course and proved himself to be as stubborn as any of his species.

One bright spark shouted: "You are going the wrong way."

"Yeah, I know," I replied, "if I could find the steering

wheel, I wouldn't be."

We still received a rosette for entertainment as did Amanda Saunders, from Chudleigh, who completed the course a lap ahead of her nearest competitor.

The stewards attempted to handicap me in gymkhanas, although the fact every pair of eyes was on me was already something of a hindrance. I'd be sent further back at the start to give the other kids a chance, or I'd be given an extra potato in the potato race.

I got better and better as I studied the gymkhana maestro, Eric Wonnacott, who was a good 20 years older than me. I thought there was no way I could ever beat him, but that was my goal and I practised and practised until I could. I would take the trippers out on rides and practise vaulting on Spotty all the way down the road. I trained him, using tit-bits to entice him to stop and run in as soon as the music was turned off, and then I'd lend him to friends for musical pole races and watch them fall off because he was so quick. When I started to beat Eric I got one almighty kick out of it. Without a care or thought in the world, I had a ball as a teenager. I was constantly accused of cheating but I was cocky and confident and I knew every trick in the book. Gymkhanas were my speciality and I reigned over the local scene until I was 15.

In hunter trials, I had one or two tricks up my sleeve, too. Most hunter trial courses involve a timed section where you have to open and shut a hunting gate. If it were jumpable, then we'd fly over. There was no rule to say you had to open it . . . and it was in the way.

If I had to open it, more often than not, the latch would be set at an adequate height for someone on a

Shetland pony so, until the timed section, I'd ride with one stirrup much longer than the other. Then I would lean over, balancing my foot in that stirrup, undo the latch, and off we'd go with my foot now placed in the leather above the iron. That was highly dangerous but fear wasn't something I was accustomed to back then. I just wanted to win.

I was a member of Cockington Riding Club, which was made up almost entirely of girls, and from the age of 11, I had a different girlfriend every week. The proviso was that they had to be blonde. My friends and I had quite a little posse and we went round the gymkhanas more often than not surrounded by females who were only too happy to help groom our ponies or plait up whilst we sat back and watched, giving them a good ribbing in the process.

Kevin Coake, Kevin Fitzgerald, Simon Innis, Paul Hosgood and I would spend our weekends competing. Paul was an orphan from Okehampton and mum and dad fostered him when he was 14. He'd first come down one summer on a trekking holiday and loved it so much he came back every year. He wanted to go to Ashburton School and the only way they would accept him was if he was fostered locally. He's been a part of my life ever since and, on and off, worked at Hawson. Now he is an equine dentist and he trains a few pointers.

*

There was good money in gymkhanas then, and like goats after the washing we never missed a competition. Mum and dad would pay the entries and I got to keep all the prize money. I could win 40 or 50 quid a day and on one of my best days I took home £65. I was pretty rich back then, especially when every show had about 20 gymkhana classes.

When I was 11, I really got going and did pretty well. I was sharp and cut as many corners as I could. I used to put grass in the bottom of my potato bucket to stop the potato bouncing and I made the unsaddling race my own. When I started, I would take off my stirrup irons and use a single girth; then somebody would copy that and keep up with me, so I had to work out the next move. So I did away with the girth altogether. I would sit on the saddle, legs in tight holding a piece of mane, and then I'd sit on the wither and push the saddle off. Once at a local gymkhana when I was 14, I was slipping off so on the way round I grabbed a girl's pigtails and pulled myself back on. We got a lot of complaints, but I wasn't doing anything wrong.

Ivor Lang was the clerk of the course at Newton Abbot for years and he and Mick Rusden judged the gymkhanas every weekend. Mick, who was often the starter, used to smoke a pipe and I could anticipate when he was going to start the race. As soon as he took the pipe out of his mouth to say "Go" I'd get a flying start. In order to give the command he had to take a deep breath. At that instant, I would kick my pony and, by the time the word came out, the boot had connected with my pony's brain, he would propel himself forward and we would have a good second's start on the others.

At Lustleigh Show, in the potato race, Ivor Lang said I was 'out', so I sat in the middle of the field with my pony and did a cross-legged strike. I said I wasn't moving until he told me why I was out and he said I had won too much. I told dad, who went to the secretary and said they shouldn't have taken our entry fees if that was the case. There was one almighty row between Ivor Lang and the organisers.

Many years later, I was at Martin Pipe's, schooling with Peter Scudamore before we went on to Taunton. It had been raining a lot, so we decided to walk the course. On the home turn the ground was really soft where they had put in drains. Peter suggested we complain because it was not fit to ride. I shrugged my shoulders and told Peter it was no good me saying anything as Ivor Lang would not take me seriously.

Before the race, Ivor came in to talk to the jockeys, told us about the drains on the home turn and advised us to race wide. I couldn't believe he was expecting us to do this on the turn for home and said, if he considered it unsafe, he should put up markers.

And he said with a smirk: "So you can cheat and run up the inside?"

He still looked at me as if I was a kid at Lustleigh Show.

My eyes caught Peter's across the weighing room. He looked stumped and I could no longer keep my mouth shut. I asked if he was seriously expecting us to race wide on the home turn and if he did, he should doll it off.

In the first race, a horse fell and they dolled off that part of the course. I often wonder what the consequence would have been if either horse or jockey had been badly injured.

On another occasion, I met Ivor Lang in the high street in Newton Abbot and asked him about the possibility of framing races at the course. I suggested they have a juvenile hurdle race for three-year-olds, with a 5lbs penalty for winners on the Flat.

He said: "You've probably got a horse you want to put in it."

That season, at Market Rasen, the clerk of the course did just that and was given a half-page write up in *The Sporting Life*. What a great idea.

*

As kids, we never wore jodhpurs and boots. We were far too cool for that. We would all deck ourselves out in jeans and bumper boots so that we could run quicker. Gymkhanas were serious business back then.

I even had an ex-pacer called The Cat for the trotting races until the judges sussed that she wasn't actually trotting, but then there was nothing they could do because there were no rules against it. My argument was that she was still doing a two-timing gait. Splitting hairs I know, but I was argumentative.

I spent a lot of time with Rod Millman, another ace at gymkhanas who now trains Flat horses near Cullompton. His father trained greyhounds at Chudleigh and we would exercise them on bikes. He would come over at weekends and we would hare through the woods together – an early introduction to our racing careers. He bought a n   ice   pony called Minnie from us. Minnie had won the Dartmoor Derby the previous year, and they did very well together.

I learnt from anybody I could and from all walks of the equine world. I was constantly trying to improve my technique and the dealer Michael Rowe, who came from near Bristol, helped me perfect vaulting onto the ponies, although he didn't realise it.

Mum got to know him fairly well through the sales. He was a successful dealer and we bought a lot of ponies from him to use in the trekking school. We also bought the mare Hold Me Tight from him. She bred Holdimclose and Hold Your Ranks, who won seven races for us at Newton Abbot in the 1990s.

Small and fairly slight, Rowe was a brilliant horseman who would be able to look at a horse and instantly say whether it had cow hocks, curbs, thoroughpins or splints. He could pick out a good horse from a bad one and I learnt a lot from him at the sales, just watching how he handled his horses, even down to how he loaded them up in the lorry.

I would often ride his horses for him up and down at the sales with them wearing just a headcollar and we'd hold vaulting competitions, jumping from one side to the other. It was a proud day when I actually managed to beat him. At that point, I knew I had the gymkhanas sussed.

*

When I was 14, the sun was beating down on a beautiful summer's day and I had work to do. Mum had bought four cobs from Mr Rowe and we put them in a field with no water supply. Usually dad took water to them in the Land Rover but he had gone away for the day with mum, so I had to think of something. I couldn't leave them there with no water because it was baking hot.

Ursula Hambley, one of our grooms, was given the task of helping me. She was 19 but she couldn't drive, so she wasn't a lot of use. But I needed to get water to the cobs and we decided the best thing to do was to take it down with dad's old cart, using another cob that had arrived the day before.

I sat at the helm, driving the cob, who was going very well until his mouth started to feel more solid by the minute. The more I pulled, the quicker he went until we were travelling at a fair old pace down the lane, which was only wide enough for a single vehicle. The milk churns carrying the water were bouncing about and we were bouncing off the high banks on either side of the cart.

I had my feet on the boards leaning flat back, pulling with all my might and didn't noticed a Rolls-Royce looming up ahead of us. I ordered Ursula: "Jump out, Ursula, and stop him."

"Oh yeah, and I'm super-woman. How the hell do you think I'm going to do that?" she screamed back.

We squeezed through and I think the car was all right, although we couldn't hang around long enough to find out. Eventually we came to a stop by ramming the cob into a hedge. And then, sweet as innocence, he went about his task nicely. By the time we returned home he was quite manageable but he reminded me of the phrase: "Milestones will tame man and beasts." If you put enough work into an animal you will eventually calm him down. We had some fun with that old cart; me, Stephen Webber, Andrew Perkins, Graham Smith, Linda Goodchild, Shirley Pedrick and the other kids from the youth club.

When Britain went into the Common Market, we all dressed up in the national costumes of various European countries, and Nobby, so called because he had two knobs where his collar had been badly fitted on his shoulders, pulled the cart through Buckfastleigh. We would put all sorts of horses and ponies into that cart and go out to the village, pick up girls and go for picnics on the moors.

Hawson Court became a focal point for all my friends. Having horses and ponies had always been a team effort, with me and mum and dad putting in the bulk of the work and my friends helping whenever they could.

*

Mum and dad were fantastic. Despite mum's prejudice against sending me to school, I was brought up well. Mum has always been my mentor and is the brains behind the show. She hasn't changed much over the years, just a little older and wiser. On first impressions she can appear standoffish, but she is essentially a very shy person who likes to keep herself to herself.

She is wary of the press and of the phone, and is set in her own little ways. It is without a shadow of doubt that I say she has exerted the biggest influence on me. She is the boss and I have never argued with her decisions, not now or ever. We have always discussed things but if she says: "This is how we are going to do this," then that is how it is done. I would never argue because, at the end of the day, I respect her. If she says no, then that's final. With girlfriends, she was always very relaxed, although she only needed to give me an approving or disapproving look and I'd know what she was thinking. If they had long fingernails, she'd say: "Not practical, that one."

"Another one for breakfast this morning," I'd shout down the stairs and then appear with my latest conquest. She would raise her eyebrows, and not so much frown as look slightly more stern than usual. "I don't approve of this one," her expression would be saying, and I knew this one would be for the elbow, which suited me because I never wanted to be involved in a long-term relationship.

If someone asks mum to train a horse, she will say: "What do you want us to do that for?" Or if someone says they want to buy a horse, she'll say: "Well that's a silly thing to do. Have you thought about it?"

It takes a lot to get mum's trust and confidence and she is not the type of person to ever wallow in self-congratulation should horses from the yard do well. She has always slowed me down too: "You can soon get into trouble by going too big and not having the money to back it," has been her driving philosophy. Subsequently she has built Hawson from just five boxes and a muddy puddle. Bloody hard working, canny and shrewd, she runs it on a shoestring and she's one of the most industrious and dedicated workers I have ever come across. She has never owed anyone anything, and, although every son is bound to look up to his mother, I have nothing but respect for my mum.

She has always been a good critic without denting my confidence, although that would have been quite hard anyway, given my naturally buoyant demeanour. I would definitely have rebelled if mum had been more authoritarian. She gave me a long rope to play with but made sure I never hung myself.

After a hard day's work we would be let loose to our own devices at night. I started broadening my horizons from the immediate vicinity of Buckfastleigh when I was about 14, and it was with great regularity that we would head to Torquay, a great place for clubs and pretty girls.

We were contracted to the language school on Torquay and we'd take 20 or so students for day treks on Dartmoor. After spending all day with pretty Scandinavian girls on the moors, we couldn't wait to see them all in the clubs in Torquay.

The only time I've ever been in trouble with a female that I can recall was when I was chucked out of a car coming home from a point-to-point at Bratton Down. Sarah Cutliffe was driving her swanky, new little sports car and, having seen an advert on TV, I put my finger on her mouth and asked: "Do you use Gillette?" She shoved me out onto the verge but it was all right because there were plenty of other people heading back in my direction.

When we went clubbing, Kevin Fitzgerald, the only one of us who could drive, would be at the steering wheel of dad's old van, which was used for his shoeing round during the day and transformed into a taxi at night. With Paul Hosgood, myself and Simon Innis, he would park up in Cockington, a village on the outskirts of Torquay, and catch the bus into town. We couldn't let the girls see us in the van.

We were pretty good in those days. We would drive along the back roads, through the villages of Staverton and Landscove, and siphon a gallon of petrol out of half a dozen cars until the tank was full. Not surprisingly, dad was always happy to let us borrow it whenever we wanted. But we were only kids and I wouldn't do it now – all the cars have locks on their petrol tanks!

I am very close to dad. He'd come into my room and give me fatherly chats and advice on my career. "I'm no good and I can't do it," I'd tell him.

"Don't worry lad. Rome wasn't built in a day," would be his reply.

Dad's patience was tireless and he always had time for me. Every weekend, he would take us to the shows in his lorry with its championship rosette in the window emblazoned with the words: "Ask the West – we are the best". As we made our way around the county, the hills came alive with the squeals of me and the lads singing at the tops of our voices. We were brothers in arms who shared a disdain for authority.

Dad doubled up as a hitching post, as we handed him the various ponies. He would give me small hints on my riding, but he largely allowed my skills to build up naturally over the course of time. He always ensured I learned from my own mistakes. When things went wrong, he'd say: "Never mind, you'll do it differently next time."

As soon as I was big enough, I went shoeing with him and it was my job to take the shoes off and keep the fire hot. I came home with a ferret on one occasion and another time it was a puppy, which was added to the menagerie. By the time I was 13, he had taught me how to shoe my own ponies.

Chapter 4

An Unnecessary Evil

Growing up surrounded by horses was a unique experience. School, however, was a different story altogether and I hated it. I started in a private school at Coombe in Holne, a village near my home, stayed there until I was six years old when it closed down, and then spent two years playing with ponies. The authorities realised I was an absentee and chased after mum and dad until they made me go back to school.

The bus would pick me up at the end of Hawson drive, which is nearly half a mile long, but often I wouldn't bother to jump on. Instead, I would spend the day playing in the woods or the fields near the road. The bus would come back again in the afternoon, and that was my signal that it was time to return home.

I had no brothers or sisters and we were a long way from the nearest town, but I wasn't a lonely child. I was immersed in my own thoughts and spent my days happily playing cowboys and Indians on my own. I had an imaginary black stallion called Black Fly and Arrow, with whom I could communicate. He was the defender of the horses and I was the defender of the Indians. It was easier for me to be an Indian because I couldn't afford a saddle and, when I did have one, I couldn't be bothered to tack up anyway. We'd spend our days in the forests behind Hawson fighting the cavalry. We always won.

Mum and dad weren't strict, and they never pressurised me to go to school. I think mum thought it was a bit of an inconvenience when there were so many ponies to break in for selling, but I was taught to be responsible from an early age. My parents put their complete trust in me, and the fact they always treated me like a young adult meant I grew up a very confident lad.

Such was their lack of concern over my schooling that, one day when I was eight years old, my uncle, Stuart Middlemass, came to the stables and asked mum where I was. "He's at school, of course," she replied.

"I don't think so – he's singing away down in the woods," he said.

Uncle Stuart, mum's brother, had ridden successfully as an amateur. He was my childhood hero and gave me the ambition to ride in point-to-points. He also taught me how to shoot and fish.

*

After that incident dad walked me to the school bus for a while, but I was never rebuked for my non-attendance and, in the end, it was nothing more than a necessary evil I had to endure on the days I could be bothered. At primary school, when I did go, I did well and passed my 11-plus exam. I should have gone to the grammar in Totnes, but I went to the secondary modern in Ashburton instead as that was where all my friends were.

I may not have always attended, but primary school was fine. However, my life and social circle would change dramatically following an incident in the summer holidays prior to starting at the big school. That was when it all started to go wrong. I was at Holne gymkhana doing my usual impressions of a speed king on a pony, and a boy I didn't know was teasing one of the village girls, pulling her jumper. I shouted: "Leave her alone."

He stood up and said aggressively: "Come here and say that."

I said: "I'll get my pony and run you over."

Lyn Prouse, the girl who was being teased, came to my rescue, we got talking and I discovered the aggressive kid liked ferreting. Shortly afterwards I was at the collecting ring and needed to change ponies quickly, so I made a mad dash back to the lorry and the same boy accidentally ran out in front of me. I had no intention of running him over but smacked him square on. From that moment, I was a marked man.

The stricken lad turned out to be Gerald Penfold – one of the toughest kids in the area. Gerald, along with his brothers, his family and a horde of cronies, including John Grant (who was the toughest, most rebellious child I had ever come across), was not the type to mess with, but there they were threatening to beat up an 11-year-old kid on his first day in school.

My ferret saved my life. I gave him to Gerald as a

peace offering and, reluctantly, I came under their wing. Thank god for that little creature because they were a seriously rough lot. It set the trend for the rest of my days at school, a period of my life I grew to detest. I was wild and uncontrollable until I left school at 16. Even once I'd left, it wasn't until I took a six-month sabbatical in New Zealand with Uncle Stuart, Aunt Sally and their children, Sam and Becky, when I was 21 that some semblance of order came into my life.

Gerald and his gang used me as a pawn. It was meat to the lions and it was carnage. I would go up to the big fifth year lads, do something nasty to them, they'd turn round to hit me and up would pop Gerald and the boys. If the teachers got involved, Gerald would say the fifth year boys were threatening to beat up a first year . . . me.

The system worked well until I was in the third year. At that point, the boys had left and I was on my own and in trouble with the older boys. But I was a big strong lad and, for the most part, I could hold my own. Uncle Stuart had always taught me to hit hard and hit first, and I had a mean punch. Gerald and I have remained very good friends. He did his farriery apprenticeship with my father and now he's a Jockey Club starter.

Even without Gerald and the boys, Jimmy Frost was a name the teachers knew from the moment I had walked over the threshold of that school. Mum and dad were so busy with the riding holidays, trekking and ponies, that they never got round to buying me a school uniform. The teachers started to put pressure on me, but they hadn't reckoned with a side of my character that has always resisted pressure. Tell me to do something and I won't do it, no matter what. I never did wear a uniform.

*

That stubborn streak, which has surfaced many times throughout my career, was the cause of further turmoil. The teachers had me singled out as a troublemaker and they were right. It came to a head in a metalwork lesson when I was 12. Our homework was to find out why horseshoe nails are made square. "At last," I thought, "something I can do. I know about horses."

Dad, a farrier, could have done the work for me but he made me read a copy of *Holmes' Principles and Practice of Horseshoeing* and study it properly. I did my diagrams to explain the workings of the horse's hoof with the square nail-head so that you could drive it into the foot through the side of the wall without splitting the hoof, which a round nail would do.

I drew meticulous diagrams of the horse's foot to show the hoof, live laminae and dead laminae and the pedal bone. I also described why it is so important to drive the nail in correctly because the hoof is not a block of wood on the end of the foot, which is what some people believed.

I thought I'd done really well and went back to the metalwork lesson, pleased with my first real effort at schoolwork, and showed everyone my answer.

"Wrong," said the teacher. "It's because the holes in the shoe are square."

There was nothing anyone could have done to suppress the rage that was rising inside me.

"You have no idea what you are talking about, and if that's what you think, you are not fit to be a teacher," I said. That's when I formed the opinion that, if one teacher can be so wrong, the others must all be too.

"You should not say that to a teacher," he countered and we had a pretty violent row. He threw the blackboard rubber at me and I threw a chair at him.

"Now I'm in trouble but I'm not waiting around here for it," I thought and went straight to the headmaster's office and told him what had happened.

That incident left quite a mental scar, and things only got worse as my school career went into freefall. I didn't want to be there and, if I went to any classes, I would resolutely refuse to lift a finger.

From the third year onwards, I did not put pen to paper, not even to write my name. It was not clever and I'm not proud of it. My parents were made aware of the trouble I was in by a couple of social workers, but it didn't help matters because I had made my mind up about school. A social worker came round to the house and she told me that it was only by staying on an extra year at school and studying that had got her where she was. I said: "Oh yeah, and where's that?"

My confidence in teachers was completely dented. Every Wednesday, about 20 students from Exeter University would turn up to ride and I would escort them across the moor. I would chat to them about their degrees and what they wanted to do with their lives and they would tell me their plans and add: "If that fails, I'll go into teaching." I formed the misguided opinion that all teachers must be failures.

Despite my reservations about the education system, I went on a few of the school trips, including a project on the depreciation value of cars. We stood on a bridge over the A38 at Ashburton and made a note of the cars that went under us, went back to school, picked a model, wrote to a local garage to see how much they were worth and then checked their value six months later, at which point we worked out the depreciation value.

However, while depreciation rates of Cortinas and Cavaliers were being calculated on the blackboard, I was causing trouble at the back of the class, racing my team of snails. Kevin Hockley, another racing fanatic, and I would have racing competitions under the table and with a tape recorder we would make proper commentaries: "And the Queen's Corgi is now running on past Andy Turnell on Birds Nest . . . "

Our commentaries became too loud and Mr Hill, our English teacher, became aware of how disruptive our behaviour was to the rest of the class. Since I'd first sat on a pony, I'd been fanatical about all forms of racing, from donkeys to pigeons. Mr Hill saw me gesturing to him. "Shut up, keep quiet and get on with your work," he said. "Come to think of it, I haven't had any work from you yet."

"No, you haven't," I replied.

"Why's that?" he said.

"Well, cos I haven't done any probably."

"What do you mean you haven't done any?" he asked.

"I don't do it," I said.

"What do you mean you 'don't do it'?" he said.

"Well, it's like this. If there's something you really have to do, you get on and do it but if there's something you don't really have to do, you don't do it and I don't really have to do your lesson," I said.

"Get yourself up here," he said pointing to a spot near his desk.

So I walked to the front. "Stand up straight," he said. "You walk as if you've got a horse between your legs."

I could not believe what he had said and felt the aggression starting to run through my veins. This was getting ugly. "That's probably because I have most of the time," I replied.

I was wearing a denim shirt and cowboy belt and heels with steel toe-clips so I could hear myself walking. My thumbs were tucked neatly in my belt and I had a defiant expression on my face. He probably thought I was being cheeky with my reply, but it was true. With a flat hand, he swiped me across the ear. He had over-stepped the mark. He offered the fight and it was like a red rag to a bull and I was not stepping down. I was sharp, fast and strong and he was quite an old man.

It broke into a huge fracas. I enjoyed fighting and I ended up hanging him by his belt to the window with Kevin's help. The headmaster wanted to expel me, but no other school would have me, so they were stuck with me.

*

I created a lot of trouble, but nothing too serious, and I knew where to draw the line. The school was very good and did its best to cope with an uncontrollable teenager. They never succeeded in making me do any educational work but I was more than happy to run errands.

The headmaster had taken me aside and told me I was

bright but that it was a shame the school had lost me. They would never drop me into the lowest grade because they knew I would have caused too much trouble in a lower class, where the boys would have followed me.

I would smash fire alarms and then say: "Believe me, I'm going to have to leave school because the fire alarms aren't working and, believe me, I don't have to be here."

Then I'd go into the boiler room and turn all the heating down so the school would get so cold that I'd have to leave because, if the temperature dropped low enough, you were not allowed to stay in school.

After the third year, the headmaster would send me on odd jobs. In the mornings my first job was to take the registers around school. I would enjoy that because I could walk in and out of the classrooms watching all my friends working hard. I would catch the bus and then I'd take the paperwork into Newton Abbot.

I couldn't read or write very well, but it wasn't until I left school that I realised that I needed to if I was to open a bank account. I couldn't have written an essay, but I was never afraid to ask and Grandma Middlemass had taught me how to use a dictionary.

Dad always thought I should work harder because he was public-school educated and would have wanted me to do better, but mum realised I had no interest in academic work and time spent at home was more beneficial because I was happiest with my horses. On one ocassion I came home and told mum I'd been thrown out of class. Mum's reaction was that I shouldn't go to religious lessons anyway because that was what caused all the wars in the world so I never went again.

I would fit school in around the ponies. Exeter Market was held one Tuesday a month, so every Monday was spent washing the ponies we were going to sell; on Wednesday I would try out all the new ponies mum and dad had bought; and there was no point going to school on Thursdays and Fridays, so that was one week out each month.

The teachers would give me a detention and I wouldn't go. Then they would give me a week's detention and I still wouldn't go. Then it would be a month. "You can give me detentions for the next three years and, when I leave school, you won't be able to do anything about it," I'd say.

The PE teacher picked up on my point-to-point career, but all he said was that it was quite good. I was a decent rugby player and was good at cross-country running, but I bunked off school as soon as Newton Abbot races was on. I regret it now and, when I'm with certain people, I do feel very uneducated, but as soon as I left school I knew I was on the right side of the law. All I wanted was to work with horses.

But with our children, Daniel, Hadden and Bryony, it's a different story. Technology is growing so fast and they have all the equipment they need to keep up with the times, but their biggest influence is my wife Nikki because she is such a good mother. She always encourages them with all their schoolwork. If it was up to me – I'd rather be playing with them on their ponies!

CHAPTER 5

What Is This Racing Game

Weighing barely eight stone, my point-to-point career was launched on 11 March 1972. Aubrey Fuller had a horse called Doctor Fred. He was a seven-year-old of unknown breeding, who was bought for 80 guineas from Exeter Horse Market, and Aubrey wanted me to ride him. So mum, dad and I set off to Lemalla in Cornwall. Even then, as I struggled to carry my weight cloth across the muddy fields of Cornwall, I was harbouring the dream of riding in the Grand National. However, if you had told me I'd still be race-riding 30 years later, I'd have laughed.

There were no feelings of fear for my first ride over the sticks. It was just a glorified hunter trial wasn't it? The fences weren't much bigger or as trappy or tricky, so I would be fine. The fact that I had made history by becoming the youngest rider to win a point-to-point never really sunk in afterwards. People were horrified that my parents were going to let me ride so young, but all I wanted to do was prove the critics wrong.

It didn't matter that no one spoke to this young black-haired kid in the changing room. I just felt really excited because I'd ridden Doctor Fred in plenty of hunter trials and I knew him well. Down at the start, I sat on my horse circling around and thinking logically about what could unfold. "There are 12 of us in this race and one of us has to win it and that winner could be me." I was very competitive and hated losing.

We jumped off and, before long, Stephen Long was hanging round his horse's neck. Mark Reeves was on a horse that was tubed, which basically means the horse breathes through a hole in his throat, and he was hunting it round. It made a noise like a steam engine and I'd stopped and listened at the start because I had never heard anything like it before and wondered what was wrong with it.

I was having a lovely time and with three fences to go I thought I'd better get going. My uncle Stuart, who had ridden at the course a lot, had told me not to go for home until we'd jumped the third-last because it was a trappy fence with a bit of a drop on it. We got over that, and I thought I'd better catch up, so I whacked my horse twice on the bum. He moved up a gear and he won. It all seemed so simple!

The saddle, all four-and-a-half stone of it, which was more than half my weight, didn't seem as heavy when we walked back to the changing room, I was walking on air and I thought the whole thing had been remark-ably easy. I crashed back to earth on my next two rides.

When I was riding Spotty, I used to have lessons in Ashburton with Major Bateman. He'd ask me what I liked best about my pony. "He's fast," I'd say every time. "Any fool can go fast," would come his reply. I thought he was wrong until I hit the deck at Buckfastleigh and those words came back to haunt me. "Any fool can go fast."

I had no idea about speed and would go flat out wherever I was – in the woods on ponies, in gymkhanas, on the moors and particularly on the racetrack. But that fall soon knocked some sense into me. It was beginning to dawn on me that winning races wasn't about getting to the finishing post as fast as you could and by whatever means possible. It was about control combined with speed. I'm not saying I adopted new tactics straight away but I did start working on it and gradually my riding started to improve.

*

My early point-to-point career took a while to get going and the following year I didn't have any luck. This pointing game wasn't as easy as it looked. Not only did you have to beat all your opponents in the race, you had to get your horses to the course in the first place.

I had a couple of horses to ride but Golden Flyer pulled up on his sole outing at Buckfastleigh and then a car hit him. His injuries weren't life threatening but it took him a good year to recover. My other horse, Stories Roma, had tetanus, so that ruled him out for the season. I asked the vet if he would be able to run the next week. "Okay to run?" he asked. "You'll be lucky if he lives."

He had a 200cc anti-tetanus jab every day for two weeks. I would sit with him and feed him porridge oats with eggs and glucose to try and keep him alive. After a fortnight, we gave him a drug called ACP to relax his muscles and managed to nurse him back. He made a complete recovery and 12 months later we won a maiden at Lemalla.

But a lack of rides didn't put me off. I loved the buzz of point-to-pointing and I took the flair I had displayed at gymkhanas onto the course. But I was no angel and got a good few people's backs up with my attitude.

For a start, if I wanted to be the best point-to-point rider in the area, I had to ensure I got as many rides as I could. The older I got, the shrewder I became at ensuring I was on the horse that could win. So trainers would phone up and I would agree to ride all their horses and often I had three or four in the same race, but the plan was as solid as the Treasury.

I nearly got caught out a few times, but Lady Luck was forever smiling at me and I got away with it by telling people to back the horse I was going to ride. Before each race, Granville Taylor, who was a real form buff and race reader for Mackenzie and Selby, would help me work out the best horse in the race and, invariably, we got it right.

I would get rides whichever way I could and even managed to take a ride off Aubrey Fuller. He had a horse called Bon Appelina who was pretty wild and would run like the clappers and then refuse at a fence. Aubrey was quite dangerous, because he would take a turn and attempt to jump the fence again as the rest of the field galloped towards him. It was a situation that happened on three occasions and I'd been half pulling his leg, asking him when he was going to let me ride her. We were at a point-to-point at Holnicote, near

Minehead, and she again refused a jump right in front of the crowd. Aubrey whipped round and attempted to jump it again. I went to the stewards and pointed out to them that this was the third time his owner had done this and that it was getting quite dangerous.

I said: "Tell him, if he does that again, you are going to call him in because you can't do that when there are horses coming towards you. If he does do it again tell him you will ban the horse so you suggest he finds someone else to ride it." And whilst I said my piece I was thinking to myself: "Now I can get the ride on it."

Aubrey asked me if I would ride her next time and I thought: "I've got myself another winner."

The stewards had duly hauled him in, which was fair enough because he was getting dangerous. We then won at Kilworthy. Bon Appelina was my 99th riding success and I always wished she could have been 100th, as Aubrey had provided me with my first ever winner, Doctor Fred.

*

I got on a horse called French Garcon at Exeter one day in the 1979 Tom Cundy Memorial Hunters' Chase. His owner John Symons, from Cornwall, came into the changing room. I said: "You will win today." He'd done really well on him, winning three times on him that season.

He replied: "I doubt it. Not with my weight on him. He's only got 10st 10lbs." He weighed nearly 13st.

"That won't do," I said. "I'll ride him for you."

"Would you?" he said and promptly changed out of his colours and told declarations. We finished a length ahead of Rose Vickery on Panmure. John won the open at the Spooners and West Dartmoor meeting at Kilworthy and I got back on him at Cheltenham, where we finished second to Mr Bunny in the Charles Turner Cup Hunter Chase. Tim Thomson Jones' mother bought him later that season and they finished second in a hunter chase at Taunton. He could have won, but they never asked me how he should be ridden, so I didn't tell them. His key was that he had to make it over the first.

I've never been scared to speak my mind and if something irked me, I would be the first to say something about it. On one occasion, I'd come back from a race at Hayes Barton at Clyst Honiton and gone straight into the men's changing tent, forgetting to weigh in, and then ducked back out again and sat on the scales.

One of the terribly efficient stewards asked: "Have you just come from the men's changing tent?"

"Yes I did," I replied.

"Well, you can't go in there. You haven't weighed in yet," he said.

"You didn't have anywhere for me to put my hat and stick, so it's your fault. I'm not putting my hat and stick in the mud," I said.

In this day and age, an explanation like that would get someone into a lot of trouble but, luckily, I got away with it, which is a good job because the owner would have crucified me if I had lost that race. In fact, I was pretty adept at getting away with a lot and I could talk my way out of most situations, which I put down to what I had managed to learn at school.

Several years later, I was at Flete Park, which is part of an estate owned by Anthony Mildmay-White. This is always a very social meeting, where there is tremendous rivalry between the members of the organising hunts – the Dartmoor and Modbury Harriers. Set in beautiful parkland, it's an idyllic place where the paddock is adjacent to a cricket pitch, and the ladies' changing room is in the pavilion. You park your car on a steep hill that doubles as a natural grandstand. In 1981, Michael Ogle asked me to ride Joe's Farewell in the hunt race. Mr Ogle was a respected owner/ trainer/breeder who lived at Skerraton on the foothills of Dartmoor. All his horses were home-bred and Joe's Farewell was the last progeny of the deceased stallion Vicky Jo – hence Joe's Farewell – and he was one of seven foals bred from his point-to-point mare Bright Reply.

I'd won on Joe's Farewell when I was 17 at Wadebridge – the same day I rode my first ever treble courtesy of Agnostic and Hariemarie. He was held in such high regard by his owner that three years later, in May 1979, we made a 300-mile round trip to compete in the Savernake Gold Cup at Larkhill – a four-mile open race. That day we were conceding a 7lb penalty incurred at the Mid Devon meeting the previous weekend, but we still had plenty in hand and he was my 11th winner of the season. He was a lovely ride and jumped well, and although Tony Harris lost his stirrup on Rock County I'm pretty sure we would have won anyway. It was a good training feat by Mr Ogle because Joe's Farewell had broken down badly at Newton Abbot in 1977 and then made a winning return in his Members' race a couple of months before the Savernake.

At point-to-points, the owner has to declare his horse 45 minutes before the race. I had arrived in plenty of time for the Members' but obviously not 45 minutes before because it wasn't up to me to declare him. In fact, I was two minutes later than the close of declarations. Unfortunately, Mr Ogle would not declare his horse unless the jockey was there. He was not happy at all and, stamping his feet, he said: "You will have to ride Joe's Farewell in the Open now."

I said: "I'm sorry, I can't because I have Armagnac Princess in that race."

I spotted Major Howard and Colonel Spencer coming out of the cricket pavilion. They were both acting as stewards that day so I said: "Could you just hold on a minute Mr Ogle," and walked over to them.

"Major Howard, I've had a bit of a job getting to this meeting today and I'm supposed to be riding Joe's Farewell for Mr Ogle in the Members' but unfortunately I arrived a couple of minutes after declarations closed and Mr Ogle hasn't declared the horse. Is there anything you can do to help?" I asked.

With a nod of his head, he disappeared into the stewards' tent with Colonel Spencer and two minutes later, there was an announcement over the tannoy: "Owing to the bad weather conditions on the moors earlier this morning, some people have had difficulty getting off their farms. The stewards have decided to put racing back 15 minutes."

*

All those years hunting on the moors, opening gates for Major Howard, had paid off. The smile was soon back on Mr Ogle's face, not least because Joe's Farewell, who had been my first ever hunter chase winner in 1976 at Wincanton, won by three lengths, beating George Welch and Hot Fancy.

At the time, my girlfriend was Catherine Harrison, the granddaughter of the actor Rex Harrison of *Dr Dolittle* fame. Catherine, who was a model and an actress, lived in London and was quite instrumental in my early education. We had a horse called Tim Dee who belonged to Michael Rowe, and on the Saturday we had won a maiden at Lemalla. The following Monday, he went into training with Billy Williams at Buckfastleigh so that he could run in a hurdle race at Chepstow. On the morning Joe's Farewell won at Wincanton, Catherine came to ride Tim Dee at Billy's and I was on Stories Roma. Tim Dee bolted with Catherine, hit a bank and broke his back. It was desperately upsetting and scared the hell out of all of us. Catherine came to Wincanton, but it was so traumatic that we couldn't join in the celebrations after Joe's Farewell's win.

Mr Ogle thought a great deal of his horses and when Joe's Farewell died later that season he placed an obituary in the local paper. "Mr M B Ogle's Joe's Farewell. Hunter 'chaser and point-to-pointer of great courage. Won numerous races including the Savernake Gold Cup (four miles) also three point-to-points this season including Dartmoor Members'. Will be sorely missed by family and friends."

Even when I was a boy enjoying the point-to-point circuit, I still got dragged into a few coups, most of the time unwittingly. In my last season riding in points,

David Greenham had a horse called Cape Race, which he was running at Bishops Court at Ottery St Mary. Originally, he wanted me to ride it and then he decided to ride it himself. He weighed out, the price went up on the board and his friends all backed him. He then went to the stewards, said he was sick and asked if I could ride it. We got beat; which just goes to show that the old proverb about cheats never prospering is true!

*

The intrigues of point-to-point are fascinating. Just like National Hunt, there is plenty of diplomacy involved. Devon Spirit was a horse I had always admired. I used to sneak off school to watch him at Newton Abbot and put 50p on him. He was a great big soft sort who wore a rubber bit and never took up the bridle. He was a hero trained by Diana Pook near Paignton and ridden by her son Keith.

In 1980 Dave Phillips had a horse called Ali's Chandy. I was at Axe Vale point-to-point at Stafford Cross on 23 April and chatted him up to see if I could get the ride. I walked the course and talked to Anthony Hartnoll on the way round.

He asked if I would ride his horse and I was tempted but then he decided to ride it himself. Dave Phillips jocked off Janine Evans so that I could ride Ali's Chandy. We were on our way around and I looked over and said to Anthony: "Thanks for not letting me ride yours. I'm on a better one here."

Ali's Chandy was travelling like a winner until she whipped round and stuck herself in the hedge and we ended up finishing fourth while Anthony won on Ruby Express.

The following season, I was jocked off Ali's Chandy because I didn't get on with her. Keith Pook very rarely took outside rides, but he took a spare ride on Easter Monday and broke his ankle. I rang up enquiring after his health and to ask whether the ride was still available, knowing Devon Spirit was being aimed at the Westcountry TV Hunter Chase Championship at Newton Abbot on 21 May. They decided not to run him because Keith couldn't ride him out, but even so, I offered to drive to Paignton and ride him out every day. I managed to get the ride. He had been such a hero of mine, I felt honoured to ride him.

Dave Phillips phoned me to see if I could ride Ali's Chandy and I told him I couldn't. He asked: "Have you got a ride?" I told him I had and he worked out it was Devon Spirit. The fact that I had been jocked off Ali's Chandy before made me even more determined to beat him. Both Grant Cann, who rode Cinbar, and Chris Down, on Integration, were trying to get us beaten and had taken us on in the race. Devon Spirit was getting really tired. It was very soft ground and he was making a lot of noise. I asked for one big effort over the final fence and Devon Spirit responded. I think he must have jumped that last fence on memory and determination alone, and he kept going on that run-in.

Every time I looked over my shoulder, I could see Ali's Chandy and Ron Treloggen gaining ground. Turning for home, we were 15 lengths clear but his legs were turning to lead and he was making a noise. But he was brilliant and kept going and won. He was one of the Westcountry's most popular horses. It was a glorious swansong for a fantastic old warrior who was in the money on 89 occasions. At 16 years old, that was his last race. To ride a horse like that back into the winner's enclosure is one of my proudest moments.

Devon Spirit won five hunter chases and 27 points and was placed 49 times from 105 starts. His only defeats that year were by our own Armagnac Princess at the Spooners meeting in the Open, and when he was beaten by another horse of ours, Princely Rifles, in the Men's Open at Lamerton. That was also the day I rode my first double under Rules, but I was lucky I kept the first division of the Maiden Hurdle on the 33-1 shot Moya Mowa, trained by dad, because he went sharply left on the run-in, bumping and hampering the second-favourite, Tudor Road, before winning by a neck.

After my first point-to-point ride, it wasn't long before I had my first ride under Rules and a year later we set off to Wolverhampton on Christmas Day. Arthur Souch, a north Devon farmer, had given me the leg-up on Love Set in the amateur riders' novices' hurdle on Boxing Day. Eric Wonnacott and I met Arthur with his cattle lorry and horse at Exeter.

I'd never been that far away from home before, and I'd never seen anything like the blocks of flats we drove past in Birmingham. Spaghetti Junction was something else; it was like I had been transported to another world. I was so naive, all I could think was: "Who the hell lives in those buildings?"

Arthur and Eric had a good bite to eat in a local pub. I stayed in the dormitory at the course. I couldn't eat anything because I was struggling to do 10st 7lbs and I hadn't a clue about saunas or diets or how to control your weight. It was freezing cold and there was a shrivelled mouse under my bed – a great way to spend Christmas night.

On Boxing Day, we took Love Set for a walk and it was great to be there with Eric. He had always been such a huge part of my life whilst I was growing up, and he had been the original king of the gymkhanas. But even so, at this stage, the thrill of race riding hadn't really sunk in. I was more excited about the brand new pair of racing boots dad had given to me for Christmas. I went into the changing room where, for the first time, I met the valets, John and Tom Buckingham. They showed me to the far left corner, where I dumped my kit, and then I went back out to walk the course. I came back and my brand, spanking new pair of boots had disappeared. I asked everyone if they had seen them and they all looked at me with blank faces.

I was lent a pair two sizes too big and went out to finish seventh in the race. Those boots never reappeared, which is something we always had a laugh about until the day I retired. "You've lost that like you've lost my boots," I'd say. Normally, you could leave a million pounds in your pocket and it would still be there at the end of the day, but not that time.

When I was 15, I was enjoying my point-to-point career and getting a fair few outside rides for people. I'd ridden my first winner under Rules when Mopsey, owned by mum and dad and trained by Billy Williams, won the Motorway Selling Hurdle at Taunton in February 1974. "There you go, I can do it," I thought afterwards. Mopsey was great. Mum had bought her from the Irish dealer Tim Horgan at the Sherberton pony sales, and we called her Mopsey because she had big ears, like the character in the Beatrix Potter books.

*

But, to me, the world stopped at Bristol and, riding along the lanes one day pondering my future, I decided I would be happy if I could ride 100 winners by the time I was 35. At that time, I'd had a couple of National Hunt rides for Billy Williams, who trained 14 horses at Buckfastleigh. Billy had said of me in an interview: "He has got a lot of incentive and plenty of courage. Some of the finer points need to be brought out in him and he needs to improve his style, even though it's not bad at the moment. He wants to get plenty of rides under Rules to make it possible"

The rides were coming thick and fast, but I never became a stylist on horseback and earned myself the nickname 'Jimmy The Wiggle', which I blame on my early showjumping career. I was a small child on big horses so, in order to get them to canter on the correct leg, I'd lean down one shoulder, which meant my weight went from one foot to the other. But once you start doing that, it's a difficult habit to crack. Although it may not have looked stylish, I had very few fallers.

There were plenty of trainers and owners who supported me, but in a funny way, I probably owe Gail Harrison more than anything, even though she only had one horse. The daughter of Neville Harrison, who was our vet for many years, Gail was remarkably good at training. I'd known her for years as she came from Ashburton and we grew up together, belonging to the same Young Farmers' Club and competing against each other as kids. Gail ruled the roost with a firm grip and she knew what she wanted – no ifs or buts or messing. She's worked as Martin Pipe's secretary for many years!

She had a lovely mare called Trentishoe, whom she'd bought from the legendary Olympic rider Bertie Hill from Barnstaple. The first time I rode her at the Silverton meeting at Clyst Honiton on 23 April 1977, I well and truly cocked it up. I was much too stick happy, got her upsides over the last, and we crashed through it. Gail was not amused and said I could only keep the ride if I never rode with a whip on her again. That taught me a valuable lesson. At the North Cornwall meeting at Wadebridge, we finished second in the Adjacents Hunts race before Gail put her away for the following season.

Trentishoe quickly progressed through the ranks. We won three of our four starts including a dead heat in a restricted at Clyst Honiton, and *Hunter Chasers and Point-to-Pointers* declared: "Would probably have been undefeated in '78, but the jockey does not carry a whip at the owner's request, which places him at a great disadvantage in a driving finish."

The next season, Gail's target was the John Corbet Cup at Stratford, which is the most prestigious novice hunter chase of the season. We went to Bratton Down in order to qualify because we had to win an open race, which she duly did. Bertie Hill, who owns the land at Bratton Down, came up and said: "Well done. I didn't think she would do that, I thought she was too small," which was pretty good seeing as he'd sold her as a point-to-pointer a few years previously.

Gail then ran her in a couple of hunter chases where,

each time, we were beaten. At Newton Abbot, in the Totnes Open Hunters' Chase, Smilbo Smaggins beat us a length and a half, and at the same track Sue Reynard's Wiener Chic beat us two and a half lengths in the Far South West Hunters' Chase.

Although Trentishoe's jumping was impeccable, on each occasion we were beaten on the run-in in driving finishes. It taught me a lot about using my hands and heels and I'm a tremendous advocate of these races, but, when Gail finally relented and allowed me to carry a whip in the John Corbet, just carrying it helped because she ran away with the race and won by some ten lengths. She went like a dream and I still have the magnum of champagne we won.

Gail then went to work for Fulke Walwyn, and Trentishoe was the only mare in the yard. She won another two chases.

CHAPTER 6

Silk Purses From Sows' Ears

In 1976, when I was 19, I thought about turning professional. With the introduction of VAT we were at a disadvantage when buying and selling cobs and ponies. My parents were really struggling with the trekking school, although dad's shoeing round always kept things ticking over. I'd split up with Catherine, which had hit me hard, so I decided it was time to leave the area. Anyway, if I became Champion jockey, it would help my parents, so I wrote a letter to Josh Gifford, asking him to employ me, although I never got around to posting it.

Some so-called experts had convinced me that I was too heavy and that I should remain an amateur. I had a chat with mum and dad and we decided to start training horses, so my goals changed and I was happy to stay at home.

We trained under permit until dad was granted his full licence in 1980. My point-to-point career gained pace as I became more experienced. Mum, dad and I also gained a reputation for picking up horses from the bargain basement and turning them into real stars. We'd study the breeding and look for the well-bred ones who had failed to show good form. We also helped a lot of old rogues turn the corner and really enjoy their racing. Dad had always maintained: "The price you pay for a horse has no relation to what they will do eventually."

Tight Turn was a reject bought out of Ascot for 350 guineas. He'd had four or five runs, but had tailed off each time because he was a tearaway. Nevertheless, he was by Avocat and we liked him. Paul Hosgood was working in the sweet factory at Okehampton at the time and every weekend he would come over to gallop Tight Turn. He had got a good feel of the horse so, when he first ran for us at Exeter in October 1985, Paul had told the 50 or so workers at the factory that the horse was going to win. He had a pocket full of fivers and tenners. He asked: "How are you going to ride him?"

I said: "He's coming out of the gate well last and I'm going to hold him there until he settles and then I'll feed him into the race. But the most important thing is that he settles and doesn't run off."

I had decided that he needed to be taught some manners in his races. But when Paul heard what I had to say, he kept the money for another day because he thought I wasn't going to let the horse win. I jumped the first two hurdles and the horse relaxed, went about his work like a professional and won at 33-1. The lads back at the factory were listening for the result on the radio. I don't know what they did to Paul when he returned without any winnings for them, but at least they didn't lynch him as he is still around today.

We had an unnamed chestnut horse who also belonged to a great friend of ours called Tim Horgan, an Irish dealer who sent plenty of horses to Exeter market when I was a boy. The chestnut had been sent away two or three times to different yards to be sorted out, but to no avail and each time he came back with the label "impossible" firmly attached to him because nobody could get him going. Could he buck!

Tim didn't want to put him down because he always believed the horse possessed a bit of talent, so in 1980 he came to Hawson Court. I spent hours with him in the long reins and on the lunge. Eventually, after he bucked me off several times, I could ride him in the barn, but I couldn't ride him out.

Two months on, I could get him a little further so I decided to prove my theory that "milestones tame beasts". I spent hours riding and hunting on Dartmoor and teaching him to enjoy himself. We established a good bond, partly because I had managed to make him see sense, but also because he was my very own racehorse. I named him Major Murphy.

We ran him in point-to-points and eventually I felt he was ready to have a go under Rules. In the Easter of 1981, I decided to take him to the two-day meeting at Newton Abbot. I entered him in a novice selling chase on the Saturday, which meant that if he won, he would be put up for auction. But I was an amateur with little cash going spare, so I knew that if he did win there was no way I could afford to buy him in, should anyone want to make a bid for him. Obviously, the solution was not to let him win.

We went about the race a little bit half-heartedly,

hoping we wouldn't get to the front and, coming to the last fence, I was some 15 lengths down in second, praying that the horse in front didn't fall because I really didn't want to lose my horse.

It stayed on its feet, we finished second, so we went back on Monday and were all out to win the Novice Chase by some 15 to 20 lengths. The punters thought I had had a big bet but I hadn't, I just really wanted to keep my horse. I had glasses thrown at me, the works, but I shrugged off the abuse. Given the choice between irate punters and keeping my horse, I knew where my loyalties lay. Then, to crown it all, the winner of the seller failed the dope test so we got first-prize money, which was rather apt as it was my birthday, 31 July.

*

Mum bought On Her Toes for 200 guineas from Doncaster Sales. She was two years old and my jumping pony was bigger. There was no way this horse was ever going to win races.

"Mum," I said, "if you manage to win with that, I'll buy you dinner." She did win the Novice Selling Hurdle at Exeter on New Year's Day in 1988 at 20-1. I never bought mum dinner.

When her racing career was over, I swapped On Her Toes for a number plate belonging to Gordon Chambers. I will give the plate, which reads DF 9851, to my son Daniel when he is 21. Gordon has since bred some nice horses from On Her Toes, including On My Toes, who won five hurdle races and holds the track record at Taunton.

Another horse we worked with was Princely Rifles,

who Denis Williams was trying to point-to-point, but was bucking all his jockeys off before the start. He was a super-looking horse and we had a full brother to him who was plagued with leg trouble, but they both had plenty of talent. We were pulling Denis's leg over Rifles and said to him: "When you get fed up with him, let us know." Before the next Newton Abbot races we had a phone call. "If you want that horse, you can have him."

A former useful hurdler, he couldn't have made a more inauspicious start to his pointing career, refusing to jump on his first two starts, so he was evidently sick of the game. I tried everything with him. I rode him in a head collar with a rubber bit, but he still wouldn't do any work. I would take him in the lorry to different places, but if he saw another horse he would plant himself.

Then I discovered that, if my lurcher came, he quite happily went about his work. I also found that if I rode him with my stirrups long and with spurs, he thought he was going hunting and I could get him to go. As soon as you pulled your stirrups up, he would put his ears back, pull his neck in tight and go back to his old ways. I always thought he looked more like a hunter than a racehorse.

After about a month, I got a bit of weight off him and ran him in a Men's Open at Morwenstow. We hunted around and finished a very bad third but at least he was going forward and he had behaved himself.

Ten days later, we went to the Lamerton Hunt's meeting at Kilworthy in a good open race. We got down to the start and I could not believe how obliging he was being. He was going so easily. We had about four horses in front of us and I pushed him on up the straight, and we won, beating Devon Spirit who was one of the best open horses around.

At the same time as Princely Rifles, we also had Armagnac Princess, who mum bought for 540 guineas at Newton Abbot Sales in 1978 to go hunting. When she first arrived, Armagnac Princess was a tearaway and you couldn't ride one side of her. She had a big ring around her cannon bone where she had cracked it and she was so nappy that we couldn't get her to leave the yard. She had an almighty buck and an attitude to match, but there was no denying the fact that she could really gallop.

The magic of Hawson eventually worked and we sweetened her up so that she became a useful little hireling. Every Saturday, she would carry a big chap called Jim Gibbs hunting. He weighed a good 15st stripped, 16st with kit and saddle. The first time I realised that she might be better than just a hunter was when I was riding a horse called Current Bun, a strapping 16.2hh pointer who had won a race the season before.

We were hunting on Dartmoor, which is tough going at the best of times, and hounds were running fast. Jim and I got left behind and we had a bit of catching up to do, so we crossed a river and started to gallop up a big hill. My horse practically died on me even though my weight, compared to Jim's, was nothing. Meanwhile, Armagnac Princess, who was only 15.3hh, was striding on like a good thing. "What the hell have we got here?" I thought.

We decided to put her into training and she soon began to make her mark. She made a storming debut in an Open at the Bolventor Harriers meeting in 1979, beating Devon Spirit. She had a mediocre start the following season before hitting form at Bowden Pillars on 15 March and then won her next two Open races.

But, even though she was winning, in our ignorance, we still didn't realise how good she was. If we had her today, we would do things a bit differently and she would have very solid claims as one of the top mares in the country. We were aiming at the Jeep/Christie finals at Chepstow in June 1981, and had worked back from that race to make sure she was at her peak. We decided to take both Armagnac Princess and Princely Rifles to the Vale of Aylesbury's meeting on 14 March 1981, which fitted in with our plans.

Katie Ellis, my girlfriend at the time, was going to ride Princely Rifles in the ladies' and I rode Armagnac Princess in the men's. All the locals from the pub knew the horses so they handed over their money and told us to back them. Unfortunately, for the bookies, they hadn't cottoned on to the fact that Princely Rifles had won the previous week at Lamerton, because the racecards had already been published, and he opened at 25-1, and was backed down to tens. Kevin, our head lad, went all the way down the line and put the money on and we raked it in after she won easily.

The Vale of Aylesbury meeting was the last time Armagnac Princess ever ran in a point-to-point. It was described in the press as the race of the season, and it was a tremendous effort when she was beaten a neck by

Nostradamus, that year's Grand Marnier winner. That was down to jockeyship because I didn't know the course as I hadn't had time to walk it.

Although Armagnac Princess had bags of ability, she was a typical mare and inclined to be very temperamental. In order to persuade her to put her best foot forward, I wore spurs on her for the Jeep/Christies Men's Final at Chepstow.

There were 12 runners in the Men's Championship of which only five completed the course. Among the 'pulled-ups' were the Lady Dudley Cup winner, Petite Mandy, and Mountain Lad, the Grimthorpe Gold Cup winner.

Armagnac Princess was fantastic. She made up a lot of ground on the second circuit to challenge the leaders in the final straight and win, going away, by some 12 lengths. That season she had won four point-to-points and was second in a hunter chase at Hereford in April, beaten five lengths by Cheekio Ora.

Armagnac Princess meant an awful lot to me and I suppose I was far too attached to her, which is folly in the tough world of racing. But her welfare came first and foremost. When she went under Rules and two years after the Men's Final, I did the daftest thing and pulled her out of a race at Ludlow after visualising a dead horse at a fence. I'd already ridden Kea that day for mum and dad in a novice chase and he fell and broke his back and was killed at the first fence in the straight. As I approached that same fence on Armagnac Princess, in my mind, Kea was still there.

We were challenging for the lead and I looked at the fence, thinking it had claimed a lot of horses and Kea had been killed there earlier. I could not face jumping it so I pulled her out. It took a lot of explaining to mum. She had probably just seen a large lump of prize money disappear. And I could not explain to the judges that I had imagined a dead horse – they would think I had gone mad. So, when she bolted up at Newton Abbot a week later, the stewards called me in. They were well within their rights because I had pulled up the horse the week before with no apparent excuse.

Despite my tête-a-tête with the stewards, that day in 1983 was memorable. I'd already been to Galmpton point-to-point ten miles away at Brixham in south Devon and won the members' race for Denis Williams on Flying Camel, who'd been on the circuit for four years and never managed to win.

Before the race, I walked out to the paddock and said to Denis: "Do you mind if I wear these?" pointing at my spurs.

"You can wear what you want," he replied. They worked!

Armagnac Princess became a real Westcountry favourite and she won 18 races for us in the end, including six races under Rules. She was a serious mare and probably one of the best of her era. She ran once over hurdles and was beaten by Baron Blakeney, and eventually we retired her, aged 13, to stud. She was the dam of Defendtherealm, who won several races for us.

It wasn't until a race was televised that we discovered her history after her breeders saw her and then contacted us. Bob Champion had broken her in and then she had a spell with Don Harrington. They thought they'd killed her one day because she was in her stable and she hit the beam and knocked herself out. The lads even went to get the knacker wagon, but by the time it arrived, she'd got up again.

You can fork out thousands of pounds on horses but the odds are staked against them ever winning a race. Helping troubled animals turn the corner, or breeding your own horses, is immensely rewarding. From sitting on a gangly four-year-old's back for the first time, to seeing him win a race, or helping an old dog realise that a job in racing is not such a bad thing.

CHAPTER 7

Time To Grow Up

As a child I'd been headstrong, and I carried this trait through into my teenage years. I lived life to the full, but when I was 21 I realised I could no longer go on living in this almost surreal world forever. I was riding plenty of winners as an amateur but I had no focus and didn't know what direction my life was taking. Mum and dad always maintained their easy-going attitude towards me, so they were happy enough because I was working at home. But I had to get away and sort things out for myself.

On the face of it, I was probably a very late developer. Immature and still very much attached to mother's apron-strings, I eventually made the break. Three days after the 1978 point-to-point season finished and, with 14 winners under my belt, I took a six-month sabbatical.

In the traditional manner of the young, I went travelling. However, my motivation was not to hit the trail and see the world but rather to sort out the direction I wanted my life to go in. I sold my cows, bought an airline ticket for £800 and, with £50 remaining in my pocket, I headed off to New Zealand where I stayed with my uncle, Stuart Middlemass, who was a professional deer hunter and fencing contractor.

I worked for my keep on the fencing lines at Otrohanga near Hamilton. But I missed the horses terribly and soon headed off to Cambridge and Kenny Brown's highly successful stable, which had supplied Derek Kent and Stan Mellor with so many winners. Kenny Brown is one of life's philosophers and he taught me a lot. Also gaining experience at the time was the amateur rider Paul Webber. We rode at Ellerslie at the Auckland Racing Club's champion jumpers' meeting and I rode a couple of times for Bill Saunders whilst I was there.

*

I got into the New Zealand way of life and soon did my bit for the local sheep community. I'd been at Kenny Brown's for two days and he left me in charge of the farm whilst he took some horses racing with his wife Anne. A flock of ewes were lambing and I was left in charge of their welfare. I went out early in the morning and there was a lamb at one end of the field and the rest of the sheep were at the other. I discovered which one was its mother and, after a few communication problems, I caught her with my steel shepherd's crook. I tethered her by her leg to a wooden post on the fence, got the lamb and let her suckle.

I stood back and admired my good husbandry, knowing I would need to leave the sheep like that for a couple of days whilst she became motherly towards her lamb. Feeling very proud of myself, I patted my dog on the head, reached for my shepherd's crook, which I'd left leaning against the wire fence, and I was knocked flat on my back as an electric shock ripped through my body. "What the hell has happened here?" I spluttered as I checked my heart. How was I to know that a wire fence half a mile away from the farm buildings would be electrified?

Stuart also hunted possums, and with a cheque for my efforts, I bought a New Zealand-bred horse, which I called Anzac, for 400 guineas. He wasn't allowed to keep the name so we re-named him The Alderman and he ran in five races and won two before he broke down.

When I came back, I knew that I wanted to train and ride racehorses. With such single-minded devotion, I could have been a banker. I could make deals, tread on the opposition and talk the talk. But rather than the world of commerce and finance, I chose to continue my life with horses.

I did return to New Zealand with Jennifer Barons, wife of the trainer David Barons, and introduced her to Kenny Brown after her husband had asked me about New Zealand and the horses there. That introduction led to the yard instigating a policy of buying New Zealand-bred horses, including the top-class chaser, Playschool, and the 1991 Grand National winner Seagram.

*

My weight ballooned in New Zealand and I really struggled with it. Although not particularly tall, I was heavy from working. I wasn't like that as a teenager. I had grown into a big lad, fit and strong from working on the farm.

When I was 16, I had a ride for Billy Williams at Newton Abbot and I couldn't do 10st 10lbs, so I went for a long run around the woods wearing dad's long wool overcoat. I was still heavy, so I went and squared up the dung heap. Then the doctor told me not to drink for 24 hours, which would help me lose a few pounds. To make up for it, I drank three bottles of lemonade after the races. That sort of regime would have any dietician reaching for the prayer book.

It's a different story now. Jockeys are serious athletes, so fitness and dieting is important. You have to have your body tuned because racing is so strenuous. Most jockeys can get round, but not all of them can actually ride a race. I'd grown up with pancakes and I'd never refuse a roast dinner, so I'd starve myself for two days, get depressed and then eat pancakes.

Luckily, eight months after I returned from New Zealand, I managed to lose the excess in a less conventional way than dieting. Bill Barons, David's brother, used to hunt with the Modbury Harriers and I would break in horses for him. A big brown one came along and I started him off without a problem.

My girlfriend Katie Ellis and I rode up to an outdoor school at Holne, which belonged to Sara Salmon who was the mother of my ex-girlfriend Catherine Harrison, to give the horses a bit of work and some jumping. Before we left the arena, I jumped off my horse to clean away any droppings and put the showjumps back.

The school is high up on Dartmoor with magnificent and mesmerising views over the Dart valley. We left our horses to stand quietly gazing into the distance and mine was transfixed by the view. I remember glancing over at him thinking he looked as if he was carved in stone. I walked over to him, looking at my feet, thinking about the lady I had to meet later at home who wanted a racehorse, and I took a stride too many. I was within his range, had spooked him and I could see the muscles tense up on his rump as if it was in slow motion. I knew what was coming and I knew I didn't have time to get out of the way. Whack. His hind toe hit me just below the nose and his heel hit below my eye. He smashed my cheekbone and I dropped to the floor. I remained conscious with my hand over my face. I took my hat off and it was like turning on a tap. The blood went drip, drip, drip.

Katie shouted: "Are you alright?"

"I need an ambulance," I said. She took off down the road screaming.

It was like trying to breathe through a sponge as I staggered down the driveway to the house. They rang for an ambulance, but the driver wasn't sure how to get to Holne, so Mum came up and took me to Ashburton to meet the ambulance. I borrowed a washing-up bowl and kept my head in that so I didn't make a mess everywhere. They took me to Torbay, where they rebuilt my face and later provided me with false front teeth. I had smashed my cheekbone and broken my jaw in three places. I had to eat through a straw, but it kept going soggy so I got the air pipes out of a fish tank and used them instead.

The surgeon was pioneering and he wanted to screw my head into a frame. He put my cheekbone back together by going though my hairline so I didn't have a scar on my face. I should have been in the frame for six weeks but lasted four and a half because I walked into a door. Six weeks after that, I was back on the racecourse again.

That kick wasn't such a bad thing. I was 10st 7lbs before the accident and 9st 2lbs when I came out of hospital. Since then, I've kept control of my weight. It wasn't as painful as you'd think it would be, but I did have one enormous panic attack when I came to from the anaesthetic.

I had a breathing apparatus in my mouth, but I felt like I couldn't breathe and I couldn't speak because I was very dry. They'd put some saline solution on it, but I couldn't get any air and I was getting stressed. I was chucking everything off the bed. My thoughts were confused and, for some strange reason, as the saline solution went down my throat, I thought they were trying to put water back through the tube and I was convinced they must have been trying to drown me. The doctor had to sedate me with an injection. The nurse in intensive care, Stephanie, has been a great help to my family and me over the years and she's a regular on duty at Newton Abbot racecourse.

Ever since that kick, I've been very wary of the back end of horses. However, I'm not disappointed that my worst accident didn't come through falling off a horse.

*

Riding as an amateur was costing me a bomb, and after I returned from New Zealand, I decided I didn't need a valet to look after me because, over there, you look after yourself. It was an experience that taught me a lot.

I had four weight cloths made up, apologised to John and Tom Buckingham, and became my own valet. It meant washing my boots and breeches but I had plenty of time to get things cleaned up again because I wasn't riding every day. I started to use the racecourse washing machine and I'd bring my clothes home wet. I would also clean my saddles and bits and pieces before I left the races.

I started to ride for David Barons and life was getting busier, but I was determined not to employ the services of the valets. However, my view changed on a seriously muddy day at Exeter after I had fallen off a horse called Cobbly Express and twisted my knee. I had used up all my saddles, which were liberally caked in mud, and I had four rides the next day at Chepstow for David Barons. One was King or Country, who was a serious horse in his day, and on whom I had won a handicap chase.

Andy, who works for the Buckinghams, was in the changing room and I was feeling extremely rough.

I said: "Andy, you wouldn't do mine for me would you?"

"No, I'm too busy," he said.

"I'll pay you for it, " I said.

"If I do them now, I do them forever," he replied.

"You've got the job," I said.

And I've been back with the Buckinghams since 1982.

The trainers will come in and shout, "Colours for J Frost," and they are on your peg waiting for you. All you have to do is put them on. As soon as you take them off, they disappear and make their way back to the trainer.

Everything is taken care of, and if you leave things behind, they turn up at the next meeting. Racing couldn't take place without the valets, and it would take a fool nowadays to be as stubborn as me. They are your friends and when the pressure is on they are always there offering you support; making sure you are clean and tidy. You can be at Folkestone one day in the pouring rain and your tack sodden with mud and, at 12 o'clock the next day at Newton Abbot, your saddle, boots and breeches are all there ready.

The rapport you have with the valets, and the comradeship with the other jockeys, is indescribable. John Oaksey once described it as "a brotherhood born of hazards shared."

CHAPTER 8

Turning Professional

Riding as an amateur was a carefree time for me. As long as I had a fiver in my pocket and a horse to ride, I was happy. I was getting about 100 rides a season and enjoying myself immensely. I would never have turned professional if it hadn't been for Anthony Mildmay-White, who put the wheels in motion for me to make the most of my skills as a jockey.

I had always looked up to Anthony, who at the time was the senior steward of the Jockey Club's licensing committee. I had hunted with Anthony ever since I was a little lad and in the hunting field he was someone I could speak to on level terms. He has always been there, offering me advice when I need it and on practical matters you would be hard pushed to find anyone better.

I'd applied for my usual amateur's licence but, instead of sending it to me rubber-stamped as normal, I received a formal letter from the Jockey Club requesting my presence in Portman Square, racing's headquarters.

I was a little bit stubborn about turning pro because, as usual, I didn't like the idea of being told what to do. However, when the licensing committee told me they were going to restrict the number of rides I had against professionals to 25 a season and take me back to a category A licence, I knew I had some thinking to do. The Jockey Club's argument was that I was taking a living away from a professional.

Then I realised, if I was taking money away from a professional, how much could I earn myself? I knew I had to do a job and here was one right in front of me. But it was never going to be easy because, although I only had two more winners to ride out my 7lbs weight allowance, when riding against professionals without my claim, it could be difficult getting established.

I was still in no hurry to turn professional, even though I was 25 and had ridden 104 winners. I hung on for a few more weeks so that I could ride Badsworth Girl in the *Horse and Hound* Cup for amateur jockeys at Newton Abbot on 9 September. It was an amateur hurdle race and had always been something I wanted to win. I'd been second on Princely Rifles and I was determined to win it with the mare. I thought we had a good chance, but again found one too good.

I turned professional and obtained my licence on 16 September 1983. My first ride in the paid ranks was on a horse called Daraheen Sniper at Exeter, trained by Anne Hext at Bovey Tracey, and my first win was on Tacova at Taunton for dad. We'd given 800 guineas for her at Doncaster Sales.

I put out a few feelers with other trainers and asked David Barons, who was training in south Devon,

Mum (Glynne) on Dragonfly at Poundsgate on Dartmoor

Dad (Richard) who for many years was a farrier for J. V. Rank

Mum and dad

*Dad (left) and mum (right)
in the early days with their
hireling hunters*

*Dad posing for the camera whilst
he shoes a horse*

*As soon as I was old
enough, mum sat me
on a horse*

My first pony Brown Eyes

Jim

Spotty, me and a couple of monkeys, the first I ever met

Me (left), with bleached hair, and Mark Lester for whom I doubled, in the film Run Wild, Run Free. *The pony was called Creamy and belonged to Diana Coaker*

Grandma Frost and me on Jersey

In action on my jumping pony, Snowstorm, at the Chagford Show

*Riding Miss Muffet III, one of mum and dad's early pointers, in
the yard*

*Me, in a white headband, as captain of the Dartmoor Pony Club
Prince Phillip Cup team*

*The day I entered the history books as the youngest rider to win a
point-to-point, aged 13, on Doctor Fred at Lemalla in Cornwall*

© Brian Smith

Me, playing a wounded scout, and The Cat, at the 1974 Devon County Show

Uncle Stuart Middlemass, who has been a guiding influence throughout my life

© Baths Photographic

Winning on The Flying Camel at Vennford

© Jim Meads

Armagnac Princess (J. Frost) and Nostradamus (Ian McKie) at Kingston Blount. Armagnac Princess was beaten by a short head in what was described as the race of the season

Me and Uncle Stuart in New Zealand

Leading up in New Zealand

Devon Spirit after winning his last ever race at Newton Abbot on 21 May 1981, aged 16

Our wedding day at Widecombe Church, 29 July 1986

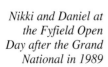

Nikki and Daniel at the Fyfield Open Day after the Grand National in 1989

Little Polveir goes over the water in the 1989 Grand National

Little Polveir (J. Frost) leads Durham Edition (C. Grant) over the last fence in the 1989 Grand National

Me, after winning the Grand National, with Little Polveir's trainer Toby Balding and The Duke and Duchess of York

© Colin Turner

Forest Sun wins the Waterford Crystal Supreme Novices' Hurdle at Cheltenham Festival on 13 March 1990

Daniel, Hadden and I on Alan Argeband's fabric stall in Newton Abbot, 1990

Michael Scudamore (right) and his son holding young Michael (right) and Thomas (left) with Nikki holding Hadden and Daniel (far left) on Dartmouth Quay

© Colin Turner

Morley Street jumps the last and wins the 1991 Smurfit Champion Hurdle at the Cheltenham Festival

© Colin Turner

Morley Street is the best horse I have ever sat on

© Colin Turner

Crystal Spirit, trained by Toby's brother Ian, wins the Sun Alliance Novices' Hurdle at Cheltenham in 1991

*Hadden is legged up for the first time in 1992. He was born on
19 July 1990*

*Left: Dad and
Daniel at
Widdecombe Fair.*

*Below: Me, Jack
Joseph and
Combermere, with
his lass Liz Vince,
after he won the
Culinaire Crudwell
Cup at Warwick on
3 March 1992*

© Colin Turner

Spinning jumps the last and breaks the course record in the Cordon Bleu Handicap Hurdle at Aintree on 3 April 1992 – the fastest two miles in my life

© Colin Turner

Spinning and Ian Balding after the win – Ian is posing nicely

Hadden (left), on his Donkey Derby speed machine Baby Blue, and Daniel off on a picnic.

My final hurdle on Bohill Lad at Exeter on 5 March 2002

Bohill Lad's owner Janet McCormack and head lad Derek McKenna

Daniel, Nikki, Bryony, me and Hadden outside the house (that Morley built)

Daniel leads the field on his coloured pony pursued by Hadden and Bryony who won't get left behind

*Hadden, aged 12,
schools over a
chase fence*

© Colin Turner

Nikki and I

*Nikki on Maggie Dee and
me on Lucky Vane out
with the Dart Vale and
Haldon Harriers*

whether he would put me up. He agreed to give me a chance and I rode my first winner for him, and my second as a professional, at Ludlow when Whenever won the Broomfield Novices' Hurdle. When I started out as a pro, it was a tremendous learning curve. I'd always been better at riding chasers than hurdlers because, in pointing, you always knew you would be riding over three miles on uneven ground, up hill and down dale.

But, for the last year I was riding as an amateur, I'd stopped educating myself and trying to improve. I felt I'd got as good as I could. I joined the paid ranks and realised I seriously had to improve and get stronger in my finishes, so my riding got better again.

I had always felt comfortable in the changing room and there was no difference really because I'd been in there often enough as an amateur. But turning pro seemed to happen so quickly and I never quite managed to carry that flair I had across to National Hunt. If I'm honest, I was a bit overawed by the likes of John Francome, Graham Thorner, Richard Linley and Paul Barton.

I missed pointing and its special feeling of camaraderie. I mean, realistically, in the depths of winter, it takes a real fanatic to endure the wind, rain and mud to watch a handful of horses run around some fields, but that was what made it special. That feeling of camaraderie was always worth it, and as the days got longer so did the atmosphere, which seemed to gather momentum until the final point of the season – the Torrington Farmers at Umberleigh.

I put a lot of pressure on myself. If I didn't get better,

I would never survive. I didn't care what I rode, I just tried to give every horse a good ride. Balance, ride out, change stick hands and ride better over each fence. I knew I wasn't that good as a jockey because I was against boys who'd ridden on the Flat who were strong in their rhythm on a horse. But I was used to getting tired pointers home, so I knew my biggest asset was getting the horse to jump.

I've never been afraid of a challenge, particularly where horses are concerned because you can equate it to unravelling a puzzle. You try and work out what is troubling the horses and then you work with it, instead of against it. You don't use force but common sense, and I think I have also benefited from a natural intuition that has been supplemented by years spent with horses.

Knowledge and a good dollop of that infamous Frost superglue got me out of most situations except for one that I remember as if it were yesterday. It probably sticks in the mind because, as I rolled over and stood up, I thought to myself, that's ten per cent of £15,000 prize money gone. Gutted! It looked like I was nailed on to win the inaugural running of the John Hughes National Trial Chase at Chepstow on 11 March 1989, on the Toby Balding-trained Glenside Jerry. Brendan Powell was on Roll-A-Joint but I was travelling better on Jerry until he unseated me at the last, having survived a much bigger blunder at the 13th. I'd committed myself and gone up his neck but, when he twisted and made the mistake, he got rid of me.

CHAPTER 9

Meeting Friends, Making Enemies

Glancing into a sea of faces, I thought I had spotted Kevin Fitzgerald's cousin, a reporter on the local rag, as he pointed up into the grandstand at Newton Abbot racecourse. Instead, my gaze fell onto a man who was to prove instrumental throughout my life.

A few days later, I was walking through Newton Abbot market and spotted the same man. I introduced myself as his cousin's friend; he shook his head and told me I had mistaken him for someone else, but still proffered his hand. That firm handshake was the start of a lasting friendship.

Alan Argeband's business is fabrics and he was attending his stall. His sideline is racing and we immediately struck up a rapport. I had just turned professional and told him Tacova would probably win at Taunton at the weekend.

The next week, I was again walking past his stand and he shouted his congratulations as Tacova had indeed won easily. We went for a coffee and had a chat and we've been talking ever since. Alan had known Jack Joseph since his childhood, and, as good friends do, they often asked each other for advice.

Mr Jack, as I have always known him, had a horse called Serena Plastics, who was a moody thing who wouldn't do an ounce of work. Mr Archiband suggested he should send him to Devon, where he could while away his time chasing sheep on Dartmoor and, in the process, sweeten his outlook on life. He duly arrived and I won my first race on him at Exeter on 27 August 1984, and followed up with a seller at Newton Abbot. The relationship was cemented between Mr Jack and myself when he went on to win a handicap hurdle at Southwell to complete a hat-trick.

By the time I retired, I had ridden 50 winners for him. Mr Jack has played a huge part in my life and is almost like a second father. He's been a tremendous support and a constant source of inspiration and guidance through the good and the bad times. I feel so privileged to have been associated with him right from the beginning.

Mr Jack has a house in Amersham and, when I was riding a lot, I would stay there. It was the ultimate in luxury and a place I really loved visiting. On a Friday night, if I had a ride at a London track the next day, I would stay there and, if I could, I would try not to ride out on a Saturday morning so I could spend a few hours wallowing in extravagant comfort. He had a masseuse and a swimming pool, and he was one of the first people I knew to have SIS, which transmitted live racing from the tracks around the country, installed. We'd spend the evening chatting about horses and going through the form book.

When it comes to business, Mr Jack is clued up and it was with no hesitation that I asked for his advice when I wanted to buy some property. It was 1986 and Nikki and I had just got married. We were living in the bungalow at the end of the drive at Hawson Court – a cosy little place had it just been the two of us, but the family was expanding. Land had come up for sale about a mile down the road, ideal for a family home, so I decided to put in a tender. At the time I banked with Barclays, but they did not want to know about my grand plans to build a new house and turned down my request for a loan.

Amazingly, the NatWest bank agreed to set the ball in motion, despite the fact I had only three grand in the bank. Contrary to everything you have ever been taught, if you ask, you do get and you keep on getting until you stop wanting. With barely two pennies to rub together, I signed for a £150,000 loan. All I had to do now was find £15,000 for the deposit.

Whenever there is a sale at Ascot or Doncaster, I always go through the sales catalogue with a Timeform book, looking for interesting horses. There was one particular filly called Diaphantine who had a very good pedigree. Having been in New Zealand, I was familiar with the breeding there and this filly's dam line was very close to Sir Tristram, a leading horse down under, so I had an idea she might be half decent.

I was stood at the sales ring side by side with Sarah Hollinshead, daughter of the trainer Reg, and we had a long look at her together. I bid a couple of times to keep her in the ring longer, and then bought her for 750 guineas.

"Great!" I said to a bemused-looking Sarah. "My £3,000 is getting smaller," and went off to collect my new acquisition.

Within a few days of Diaphantine arriving at the yard, I had a phone call from out of the blue from Norman Lake who owned sports shops in Torquay and who, for many years, had horses in training with Billy Williams. He wanted to buy a horse, liked the look of the filly, and bought her for £3,000. She turned out to be a shrewd buy and was as tough as teak. She was second five times, including to three Cheltenham winners.

A year later, on 1 October 1987, and just five years old, she won the seller at Taunton by the shortest of distances. But I had hit her 22 times to get her there and the stewards took a dim view on this. Fifteen years later, I would agree with them. They were clamping down on excessive use of the whip, called me in, looked at the video and fined me £100 for "improper riding and excessive use of the whip".

Norman moaned at the time: "I've just had my Torre Sports shop window done for the 22nd time, the auctioneer thought I had bid 1,000 guineas and Jim gets this fine." I knew how he felt!

With an additional loan from Mr Jack, I had secured enough money for the deposit on the land. I sold our bungalow and a field, and the price was reduced by half. We bought the 75 acres, and, with Mr Jack's help, we worked out a mortgage big enough to build a house, which sits in a secluded valley of its own, and houses my three kids, wife Nikki and an increasing menagerie, from horses to hamsters.

I'd look at other jockeys decked out in gold rings

worth a fortune and with their top-of-the-range Mercedes out in the car park. In their pockets, they had so much cash that they gave it to the valet John Buckingham for safekeeping. They'd go to top London clubs, had money rolling out of their ears and were enjoying a great lifestyle.

I had 20 quid in my pocket, a diesel car in the car park and yet I'd ridden more winners than them. I was near the top on 'prize money won' and yet I could not afford their lifestyle. For a young family with a large mortgage, we certainly had to trim the fat. Mr Jack put things in perspective.

"Mr Jack," I said, "How can I live like them?"

"You could do that, but you've got a big mortgage. Give it 20 years and see how life is then," he said.

His words stuck. It kept the millstone round my neck and taught me not to be frivolous with money, although at the time it was like telling a child that the best years of his life are at school, but you never realise that until you grow up.

On race days when I was riding, Mr Jack would tell me to stick my finger under the saddle so that I didn't come off. I always thought that was a bit odd. It was all right for him to say. He'd been in the army and they ride like John Wayne.

He'd have his own way of cheering me up, especially if my luck was out on a wet day after two fallers and I was feeling down. "Have your stick in your left hand if you are off and your right hand if you are not," he'd wink at me. As if I had any chance of winning!

We have pulled off a couple of gambles. Mr Jack takes the horses home, trains them himself, gets them down the handicap and then gives them back to us. Of course, we've had a couple of tiffs over the years, including once when he jocked me off Combermere after I put up 2lbs overweight at Southwell on a filly called Play The Blues. I didn't tell him and we were beaten. So I missed his next race at Ascot in 1992, when he won the £38,000-added Charterhouse Mercantile Handicap Chase.

Mr Jack didn't tell me I was being jocked off, he told mum, so I wrote a letter to apologise. Peter Scudamore rode him on his next start, the *Racing Post* Chase, where he was beaten out of sight in a race won by the Kim Bailey-trained Docklands Express with Anthony Tory up.

Then Mr Jack phoned me saying I could ride him again. Bide your time and it all comes out okay in the end. So he only banned me for a month and, in March, we won a handicap at Warwick. Mr Jack commands my utmost respect and it never really bothered me that he took me off his horse, probably because ultimately I'd been in the wrong for not telling him I was putting up overweight.

But there are some owners who have really got up my nose in the past and none more so than Terry Warner. Mr Warner had bought a half share in a horse called Sportsnews, which I had won a couple of races on, and I was booked to ride him in a handicap hurdle at Taunton.

The key to this horse was to hold him up very late, which I did and we subsequently won. I was booked to ride him again at Taunton. Tony McCoy was on Little Tora, another hold-up horse, and as we came to the last, it all got a bit ugly. I leant on Tony, who still managed to beat me a head, and I got a two-day ban. At the weights, Little Tora should have beaten us by 10 lengths but despite the fact we only just got beaten, Terry Warner was not happy and questioned my riding ability. Two days later Ron Hodges, Sportsnews's trainer, received a letter from Terry Warner stating that I was never to ride a horse for him again and, if I did, he would remove all his horses from his Somerton yard. It was all very over the top.

Mr Hodges phoned and asked if I would like to see the letter.

I said: "No thanks I can't be bothered. If he thinks that, there is no point me seeing it all on paper."

A week later, I was at Hereford and Philip Hobbs had a horse running for Warner with Tony McCoy booked to ride. His colours then were different to now and had a lot of white on them. The valet was tying Tony's silk and I grabbed a black marker and said to him: "You can't feel anything and don't look round."

I wrote right across his back: "Terry Warner is a shit." I felt fantastic.

Tony stood in the middle of the paddock and Mr Warner could not have missed it. I don't know if he realised it was me who wrote it. His horse didn't win and he had to get a new set of colours.

*

Mr Jack is a different cup of tea altogether; if only all owners were like him. He knows his horses like no other owner I know. He studies their races and also each horse's mentality, and he'll work out how each horse's race should be run. The David Elsworth-trained Kingswood Kitchens wouldn't jump if he got into a bunch of horses and he had to be kept wide. Now he will say: "Remember Kingswood Kitchens? Well, you have to ride this horse the same."

Over the years, Mr Jack has had a lot of horses with us; but the best horse we have ever had is Combermere, who he picked out of an Ascot Sales catalogue on his breeding.

To look at Combermere, you would not have touched him with a barge pole. He was small and weak in the front pasterns. When he walked, his ergots almost touched the floor but he was a full brother to Life Guard, who had won a lot of races for Mr Jack and had been my first ride in the Triumph Hurdle, so we bought him as a three-year-old for £4,800, which was a middle of the road price for that particular sale. "He might be lucky and win a seller," I told Mr Jack.

When I started him off, I thought he probably wouldn't even manage that, as I could not get him to jump a hurdle. But he gradually got the hang of it enough to go racing and began his career at Exeter on 16 September 1987 in a novice hurdle race where he virtually refused the first flight, cat-leapt the second, and eventually got going to finish an uninspiring sixth. Five days later, he improved to finish second at Plumpton.

Never let first impressions taint your judgement because Combermere turned out to be the best horse we have ever trained. Something clicked and he adored the game. We had a quiet run at Cheltenham two weeks later before he made all and won the Riverdale

Novices' Hurdle at Kempton in October.

Then we experienced our first taste of televised glory with a double at Ascot. Combermere led the field home in the Binfield Novices' Hurdle and Norman Lake's five-year-old, The Bakewell Boy, edged home by a neck to win the EBF Novices' Hurdle on 28 October 1987. A month later Combermere won the Northern Junior Hurdle at Haydock, beating Daffodil a length, and Mr Jack was full of praise for my parents.

"Everyone told them that they would not do anything with Combermere because he was too small, but they have done really well with him. He is so keen and eager," he said.

That run earned him a 50-1 quote from William Hill for the Triumph Hurdle but he bruised his foot and couldn't run. I think he would have won it because Ikdam did and we'd beaten him before. He just kept improving all the time and finished second in the Glenlivet Anniversary Hurdle at Aintree in 1988 instead.

Combermere was a huge favourite in the yard. He had the heart of a lion and anyone could ride him. But the poor little chap couldn't eat if he was turned out because he was very parrot mouthed. He had a two-inch gap between his top and bottom jaw and, when he was a two-year-old, he had been hit in the mouth by a lad with an iron bar so he only had two teeth on one side. But he was such a kind, genuine horse he never became head shy. He never had a big holiday in the field because of his problems, but the lads cut plenty of grass for him and Liz Vince, his lass, was devoted to him.

He was never top class but he was a very good handicapper. The biggest blow I have ever had during my career was losing Combermere in the Scottish Grand National at Ayr on 11 April 1992. It was far worse than being jocked off Morley Street. I walked into the changing room that day and it was hard to hold back the tears. There had been a few as I made my journey back from the course. I would have thrown my saddle across the weighing room that day and said: "Fuck it, if that's what you do to horses."

He'd been in front, jumping brilliantly, as he always did, and Captain Dibble had taken the race on and headed us at halfway and we were back in third. He was little more than a pony but every take-off was perfect. At the second-last, he took off, cleared the fence, landed and was off again. I'd gone to drive him away from the fence, as you usually would, and he'd collapsed behind, another stride and again he collapsed and it was obvious he'd lost the action on his off hind.

I pulled him up and got him to the rails and he was kicking badly, his leg severely broken. I held him saying: "Good boy, you're okay, you're okay, don't worry about it."

The vets came and put the sheets up. I held him until the gun was about to fire and then turned my head – I couldn't see him die. It misfired the first time. What a terrible way for him to go. Again, I held his head to calm him down as the vet took a second aim. I loved that horse and had formed a special relationship with the little fellow.

Liz Vince, his lass, took a long time to get over it. She left the yard for a while because she kept seeing reminders of him around the yard and found it very hard to live with. Racing is a tremendous leveller. You weather all those troughs and depressions for a few moments of joy. The Queen Mother once said something about racing being "80 per cent disappointment and 20 per cent maybe", and there is an awful lot of disappointment, but the injuries are the worst thing to get over.

After losing Combermere, I really didn't want to go on. With animals, they are born, you grow them up, they become your partner and you are a team. They grow old gracefully, they retire, and you put them down. That's fine because they've had a good life. But when they have injuries on the racecourse, it's heartbreaking. Combermere was a big one to get over. Some people will say he died doing what he enjoyed. It's hard to accept the fact that, just five minutes earlier, he was so full of joy, having the time of his life and then he was gone. And that has to be the most difficult thing about training horses – the injuries and the deaths.

That day, I flew back with Nigel Twiston-Davies and Peter Scudamore, who had won the race with Captain Dibble, and I felt embarrassed at my loss because they should have been celebrating.

At home, we planted an oak tree in the field where Combermere spent his summer holidays. All the horses who have been killed in racing have a plaque on a tree closest to where they last galloped. Clear Idea was a cheap horse bought out of a field at the back of Plymouth and he was the leading horse at Newton Abbot. He was always a bit nappy and there was one place at the bottom of the schooling ground where he liked to mess around so, after he was killed at Taunton, where he broke a shoulder, we planted a conker tree there.

CHAPTER 10

Let's Do Dinner

By 1989, horses at home were going well and we had our first live contender for the Cheltenham Festival in The Bakewell Boy. He belonged to Norman Lake, to whom we had sold Diaphantine three years earlier.

Bought for 480 guineas as an unbroken three-year-old, because his previous owner decided he was unmanageable after being kicked out of his box, he was one of our typical bargain basement cheapies who go on to become a star. The kind of horse we seem to have an eye for.

His hurdling career was promising and on his first run on 13 October 1987, he finished third to Jenny Pitman's Privateperformance at Newton Abbot. Two weeks later he won an EBF Novice Hurdle qualifier by a neck and then, as a seven-year-old, we sent him chasing. He hacked up on his debut at Exeter, a race I have now won seven times and take tremendous delight in winning. He won again at Newton Abbot, beating Forest Ranger by a length and a half, and then won the

Scilly Isles at Sandown in February by a head. That was some race. At the Pond Fence, he was 15 lengths down and just kept going.

The three-mile Sun Alliance at Cheltenham was our target, but big-race glory wasn't to come to our yard. After winning at Sandown, he slightly strained a flexor tendon. It was a bitter blow for us because we were confident of a big show. A win at the Festival would have done the yard no end of good. The Bakewell Boy was a good horse for a small stable to have.

He eventually made a full recovery and in 1990 Mr Lake wanted to run him in the Gold Cup. I felt the Cathcart would have been a better option. I was on Kildimo for Toby Balding, so Steve Smith Eccles rode him. He pulled up outclassed. Then, out of the blue, Mr Lake said he wanted to move him and he was sent to Menin Muggeridge, where he ran just once. He had always suffered with bruised feet and Mr Lake's reason was that an all-weather gallop (something we didn't have at Hawson) might prevent the problem.

We were very disappointed to lose him. However, I was able to keep up to date with his progress because Mr Muggeridge's farrier also shod Toby's horses. When I was at Fyfield, I'd ask how The Bakewell Boy was getting on. He told me he lived in bandages most of the time. After his very first run with us, he did get a slight tendon strain, which always needed to be managed carefully. Unfortunately, he broke down on his first run for his new yard.

I never asked Mr Lake about his decision – let sleeping dogs lie – and he is still a very good friend and has horses in training with us again. In racing, I'm afraid people always think someone else can do better and they're quick to move their horses.

In the late 1970s we had a horse for Harry Sibley from Bude called Glenglush, and he had a mouth like absolute cast iron. He was bought very cheaply at Newton Abbot Racecourse. We took him to Kilworthy, where I had had eight rides and he was my last one. Trying to get him down to the start was awful as my arms and muscles had given up by that time and I was really struggling. In the race I decided there was no way I was going to try and hold him, I'd just let him go. He went like the clappers and after a mile he blew up.

I rode him a few more times before I worked out the knack of keeping him controllable, and I eventually ended up winning a maiden point-to-point at Crimp on 7 May 1979. The point-to-point form book said: "Infinitely calmer in the new stable who did extremely well to succeed with a horse who defied professionals."

We later found out a bit of history on him and it turned out he'd been in training. He'd run at Ludlow and, coming down the home straight, he'd done a U-turn, gone under the rails, lost his jockey and ended up on the railway line. He went about four miles and his lad had to catch a train and go after him.

I rode him a few times under Rules and he was second in a good race at Wincanton. John Francome, cruising to my outside, looked down at me and said with his smirky smile: "You are only racing yourself, you know." He was right. It was only years later, when I sat on horses like Morley Street, that I could do the same. "This is what you call a racehorse," I'd say.

We had done really well with Glenglush and then his

owners phoned and said: "We think he deserves a better chance in racing," and sent him to Jenny Pitman. He frightened every lad in Lambourn and no one would ride him.

But things like that never dent your enthusiasm because it was the owner who made the mistake and the horse never did as well as when he was with us. My confidence was still riding high. Things at home were going well and I was riding plenty of winners for Toby.

I suppose the other jockeys must have seen me as being a little bit agricultural, although the weighing room always had a tremendous bond. I was never lured by the hedonistic lifestyle of the jockeys who live closer to the hub of the action, primarily because there was always so much work to do at home. Nevertheless, I always knew what was happening in the most intimate detail.

*

Life as a jockey is somewhat surreal and it's every bit as wild as they try to deny. The girls that lead up the horses are better known than the horses that run, and if the lads have seen any action, you can bet those walls of the changing room will know every detail. If they could talk they would tell enough stories to fill a book of the bluest hue. Days after the weekend were always particularly good with plenty of ribald stories flying around.

Me and Steve Smith Eccles had a strong friendship right the way through. I'd get a phone call from him saying: "Frosty, it's the Ecc, we're going to the Palace in Torquay tonight, can you fix us some entertainment."

I'd phone whoever was available and find entertainment for the night. I could always find a few locals keen for a night out and the Ecc would never miss an opportunity – not many jockeys do.

In 1986, it was frozen before Cheltenham and John Edwards sent Pearlyman to do some work with the Messer-Bennetts who have a small point-to-point yard on the north Cornwall coast. Paul Barton, John Edwards' first jockey, and Robert Kington came down with the horses and wanted to meet up for a night out in Plymouth.

Like moths around a lamp, they pestered, they got singed, and they flew back for more. They tried very hard with just about any female they could find, but kept getting turned down – hardly surprising as jockeys are not usually the best-looking lads in the world. We are fine if we are amongst the girls who are bowled over by the racing world, but not with smart town girls.

But those two weren't quitters and we ended up in a wine bar. There were two quite nice girls, who obviously weren't from Plymouth because they looked better class, and were expensively dressed. Paul went over, they blanked him, and he came back. This happened to Robert too, so it was my turn.

I eventually went over, sat down and started talking to them. Now, it was lucky I asked them where they had come from. They lived in London, and, when I said I came from Buckfastleigh, it turned out one of the girls had a sister called Lucy who was friends with a friend of mine called Harriet Harrison and they used to go to the Grasshopper at Ashburton.

I sat there for about half an hour, bought them some

drinks and eventually went back to the others. I have never, to this day, told them why they talked to me and not them. The Devon lad had got one over on them. By that time, I had met Nikki and I'd got over the urge to pull anything available, so I left them to it. And anyway, you'd just end up with a bad head trying to get a taxi home at 3am in the morning.

*

Meeting Nikki was the best thing that has ever happened to me. On Sunday nights, Paul Hosgood, Gordon Chambers and I used to meet up at a pub called the Manor in Christow. Nikki's parents owned the pub, and she waitressed there, so the first time I met her, I spent the evening taking the mickey out of her. It was all a bit of fun but she stuck in my mind and so I decided I would return one evening on my own. But my timing was bad and she had gone to work in Austria for a few months.

In the meantime, her father bought the East Dart Hotel near Princetown on Dartmoor. I became quite a regular, hoping that Nikki would be there. She eventually came back and we started seeing each other.

I'd had a bad day at Umberleigh point-to-point where I had gone for a day out having turned professional. I thought things would be just the same as when I rode but after the last race I thought I didn't belong there anymore from a social point of view so I drove back to the pub, waited for Nikki to finish and then took her for a night out in Plymouth.

After about four dates, I was sitting drinking coffee leaning against her Aga in the East Dart's kitchen at about 12.30am, when a friend suggested we drive up to the moors. But when Nikki was working she wasn't allowed to leave until everything was done and done right. So I'd help out when I could and once washed up for a coach load of 90. Before I met Nikki, I couldn't make a cup of tea.

We eventually got away and the others disappeared into the dark. Nikki said she knew of a place on the river where we could swim. "Great," I thought, stripping naked. I jumped in the river and trod water in anticipation of what might happen next. Nikki jumped in and I was about to move in for the kill, when I realised she still had all her clothes on. Talk about jumping the gun.

Nearly a year later, I wooed her on Crete and asked her to marry me. That holiday, with Paul and Nicky Barton, Colin and Anne Brown, Simon McNeile and Sarah Reeves, counted as our honeymoon and we managed to fit a wedding in between the racing and horses on 29 July 1986.

On the morning of our wedding, I schooled a horse called Chain of Reasoning, belonging to Mr Jack. Poor Nikki was dumped right into the racing world. She must have wondered what she had done. My birthday was on 31 July, while Newton Abbot races was on 1 August and Chain of Reasoning won.

We've been together for 16 years and she has been a fantastic support and a wonderful mum to our children. We are lucky because she has never interfered with the racing so we have never got our wires crossed. She is very motherly and maternal and she really enjoys the children. When Daniel was born in 1988 she'd bring him racing but soon gave that up after he was sick over her once too often, having eaten too much greasy food on the racecourse.

Unfortunately, none of the others we went on holiday with to Greece managed to keep their partners, except Simon and Sarah, and I tell all the jockeys now their ambition should be to remain single at 40. All you need is your saddle and your car and the last thing you want is to be thinking you've got someone to speak to or someone worrying after you. In today's tough world of jockeyship, you have to be totally focused.

CHAPTER 11

Cinderella Land

"Put Jimmy Frost on, he takes a lot of unseating and he's got long legs and no brain," my great friend Alan Argeband had advised Toby Balding when he had contacted him in search of a jockey for Lucky Vane. It was a phrase Toby came to adopt after he plucked me from relative obscurity in 1986 following a phone call that came out of the blue one autumn morning.

"Toby Balding here," he said. "Would you ride Lucky Vane for me in the four-mile chase at Exeter? The condition is if you ride him there, you ride him all season, with the long-term objective that he runs in the Grand National."

Lucky Vane had been sidelined since slicing off a heel and badly damaging a tendon in the 1985 Grand National. He had a reputation for making the odd earthquake blunder but I accepted the offer readily enough and, on 31 October, turned up at Exeter racecourse to ride him in the John Tilling West Country Challenge Trophy Handicap Chase. Thick mist had descended on Haldon Hill just before the race, which was bad luck for the racegoers but, for me, it was a blessing in disguise.

We made two bad mistakes down the back straight and, at one point, I was hanging around his neck, but the commentator, crowd and, more importantly, Toby's wife Caro were oblivious to the blunders. They couldn't see further than the second fence and I returned to the paddock, having finished third to Fitzherbert and Brendan Powell, grinning from ear to ear and patting the horse profusely.

"How did he go?" asked Caro.

"Absolutely brilliant, didn't make a mistake all the way round," I replied, and the foundations for a relationship were laid. From that day, I was to ride a winner for Toby every year, with the exception of 1997, and my final victory for him came on Jimmy's Cross in the Come Summer Racing at Newton Abbot Novices' Chase in June 1998.

Lucky Vane was inclined to flatten his fences when he was asked to really run, but we struck up a rapport, and in November we won the Surrey Racing Handicap Chase at Sandown, which proved an emotional win for Toby and Caro. They had worked miracles patching him up although they were both generous in their praise of me. "Much of the credit must go to Jimmy Frost," Caro had said. "He is a very good horseman who has struck up a relationship with the old chap."

Lucky Vane had a mind of his own and sometimes he would take no interest in his racing, so that winter he came to us for a month and I hunted him on Dartmoor to cheer him up. He went back to Toby in March to put the final touches to his National preparation, but he bruised his foot two weeks before the race and couldn't run.

After Combermere and The Bakewell Boy's double at Ascot, Julian Wilson gave me my first ever interview on television. He said the highlight of my season must have been riding Lucky Vane in the National. "It would have been, except he didn't run," I replied. He ran in four-milers for another season, but didn't do much good.

That horse was the turning point in my career and it was through him I was given the leg up on Bishops Yarn and Sheer Gold. Eventually, Toby offered me a retainer with the yard, just before Kildimo ran in the 1988 Whitbread Gold Cup at Sandown. He wanted me to ride his chasers for a year whilst his stable jockey, Richard Guest, gained experience.

I came home, discussed the offer with my parents, decided it was a good opportunity, and accepted. Graham Bradley had lost his retainer with Kildimo's owner Lady Harris, so he became the first ride of the new agreement.

Coming to the second-last in the Whitbread, I thought we had the race won and, on the run-in, Kildimo went a neck up, but that famous Sandown climb is a place for none but the brave. Kildimo just folded up and Desert Orchid kept fighting. He was a true champion. The reception that greeted Desert Orchid and Simon Sherwood was deafening. It was a magical experience just to be there.

*

The retainer was a working-man's agreement and no cash changed hands, although Toby had always promised he would give me some one day. I'm still waiting!

Lucky Vane became such a significant part of our lives that Toby eventually gave him to us. In the autumn of 1988, he came to Devon for good and became Nikki's horse. We pointed him for a season and then he went to Gordon Chambers at Wallaford Farm, in Buckfastleigh, to keep his youngsters company.

Toby is the ultimate professional and he knows his horses inside out. Whilst he very much left the running to me, he was always insistent that they were all given a smooth passage. He wanted them to finish full of running and always keeping out of trouble if possible, passing tired horses so they went home with a good memory of their race and feeling good in themselves.

Toby is renowned for identifying new talent. Tony McCoy, Adrian Maguire and Richard Guest are some of the top jockeys who began their careers in the schooling paddock behind the house in Hampshire, to the sound of a cracking Long Tom and Weenie the yapping terrier.

Those schooling sessions were brilliant. Every Monday morning, Toby would stand like the grandmaster, armed with his hunting whip, a voice that could carry across the gallops at Kimpton two miles away and with his trusty hound at his heels.

If some poor Irish lad, just weaned from his mother's apron-strings, fell off and lay winded, Toby would stride over and stand towering over him. Cracking his whip, he would shout: "Get on your feet. You've got hands like a shovel. Now go and catch that horse." The lad would lie prone, asking dear sweet Jesus what had he done to deserve this, and Weenie would be biting him for good measure.

Thirty horses would turn out on an average schooling morning and I would normally ride the novices, with two lads in front of me to give me a lead. If we weren't in exactly the right place, or were slow off the mark, that voice would come bellowing across the field and hit you like a knee in the groin.

"What the hell do you think you are doing? Come on Frosty the Snowman – get it right next time," he would shout.

At breakfast time, I would dive into the sanctuary of Caro's kitchen. A hen would come in at the same time every day and lay her egg in a special holder, the parrot would join in the banter, and Caro would give me motherly advice on everything from women to money and horses. But, even on a good morning there was always Weenie to contend with. Once a smart white terrier, he was now lemon in colour, old and cantankerous, and Fyfield was his domain.

When the Baldings moved from Fyfield to Kimpton at the end of the gallop two miles away, Weenie had been forgotten and left there. We weren't the best of friends, but still it was my job to collect him from his chair in the office where he presided over the day-to-day running of the yard and persuade him into my car.

Nothing could seduce him into that car. If I picked him up, there was a good chance I might lose a finger. Milk and sausages from the fridge weren't working, so I admitted defeat because there was no way I was going to pick the snarling beast up. For the first time, I had been beaten by an animal and decided to make a phone call for back up, but as I did so, he jumped off the seat and into the car.

He was the source of much hilarity for Toby, especially when he crouched in the long grass beside the all-weather gallop and then leapt out at the horses, barking. "Weenie!" Toby would holler, with a smirk on his face as we galloped by, holding on for dear life as the horses did what only came naturally to them; flee as fast as they could from that monstrous creature.

Fyfield was like Cinderella-land. It had a magical feel and was such a happy place with no rowing or bad feeling. We were all quite happy to toe the line even though we were often subject to Toby's wrath. If he hadn't become a trainer, his voice would have stood him in good stead as a sergeant major in the army. He commanded nothing but the utmost respect from us. There were times, however, when I did wonder about a more devious side to his character. On two occasions he stitched me up and there were a couple of times when he really got to me.

I'd been taken off Romany King after I could get no further than fourth in the EBF Novices' Hurdle Qualifier at Wincanton in March 1989. A month later, Guesty won the Haldon Moor Novices' Hurdle at Exeter by a good margin and I was so annoyed because the horse did not have enough speed for two miles around Wincanton, but Exeter was a different type of course and suited him because stamina was his forte.

But one thing Toby had always taught me was that I was a professional and so should act like one, so I bit my tongue and said nothing even when it was his fault I got slapped with a £500 fine for making a cock-up and riding the worst race of my life.

In November 1990, Toby had phoned up and told me I was to ride Romany King again in the Vickers Bookmakers Handicap Chase at Newton Abbot. With the Trevor Hallett-trained Butlers Pet, he was the 5-2 joint-favourite, but he had cut himself a few days before the race and had missed some work at home. Toby didn't think he was 100 per cent straight and had subconsciously put doubt in my mind as to whether he was fit or not. For once, I was riding with the horse's welfare in my mind, rather than just getting on with the job. Instead of riding him on, I was riding him half-heartedly. I rode very gingerly.

He was travelling so easily at the water and I was still holding on to him, scared he was going to blow up at any time. So I kept taking a breather. I consequently didn't get at him enough and we were beaten. His owner Leslie Garret was sympathetic and generously paid the fine.

To the onlooker, it looked like I had stopped him. I'd held him up for as long as I could but we made such rapid headway near the finish that the stewards spotted it. Nigel Hawke won on the David Barons-trained South Pool and we finished four and a half lengths back in third. Toby and I were sent to Portman Square and fined £500 each. I really regret doing that and should have just let him win because it's a reputation that sticks with you. But at least the horse went on to have a brilliant career and the guv'nor kept the horse.

There are times when the punter must really wonder about racing. Dad had a horse in training called Earl Hansel who had no form at all. Phillip Johnson, a good

7lbs claimer, was working for us and dad put him up in a novice hurdle at Exeter on 21 September 1988, because he knew the horse well. I was riding Malicho for Toby. We had won by some 25 lengths the week before at Hereford and were the odds-on favourites. I said to Toby that I thought Earl Hansel could win because I knew he was working well and we were giving him a stone. He beat us two lengths at 20-1 because the weight really told on Malicho. Any cynical-thinking punter would believe they had been turned over and you can't argue with that, but it was a straight race. It was incredibly embarrassing for me as I'd only just started working for Toby.

Toby's bark was worse than his bite but there were times when he really pushed me to the limit. "If you ever want to win a big race you are going to have to get a bit more serious," he would shout on the occasions I annoyed him. He always tried to fire me up before a race. "You are bloody useless – you couldn't ride a donkey down a beach," he'd say.

If I have a criticism of myself, it's that I've always been too laid back and Toby saw this in me. He knew that, on serious occasions, I needed a kick up the backside and he was the only person I have ever accepted this type of treatment from. I must admit, I probably did ride better when I was wound up.

Chapter 12

Famous Colours

My association with Toby Balding's brother Ian and Park House Stables at Kingsclere was another happy and lucrative period in my career. When I was schooling at Toby's one day, the phone rang and it was Ian, asking if I would go down and school some horses for him.

It was a fantastic arrangement. After I'd finished at Toby's, I'd drive 20 minutes down the road and school at Ian's. My loyalties very much lay with Toby, although I always appreciated the quality of horses that Ian ran. Whilst Toby was very much a father figure to me, in whose company I always felt happy, no matter how many times he told me off, Ian was slightly more on edge and he always put you under that bit more pressure.

It was fascinating going to Ian's yard, a real old-fashioned place that had evolved over a couple of hundred years. For me, the Flat horses were an interesting part of the set up and there was the added attraction of a very pretty secretary who wore tight jeans and silk shirts, although I never got a look in whilst Brendan Powell was around. Brendan had become a very good friend and if ever there were any luck going free, he would always be the person to catch it.

One morning, he had come over to Ian's to ride his hunter in order to give me a lead over the fences on Crystal Spirit. Ian was away at the time, but he had made sure Brendan filled his car with petrol as a thank you present. We went out onto the schooling ground, left to our own devices.

Chelsea, Ian's lurcher, decided to join in the fun and games and ran in front of a fence, Brendan bowled him over, breaking the fence in the process. Not only had he injured the dog, broken a fence and got his car filled with petrol, he also went away with a date with the secretary. That's Brendan all over!

Ian had just three jumpers in training and sent out two of them to win at Newbury on 24 November 1989. It was also the first time I rode for him. Calicon won Division One of the Freshman's Novices' Hurdle, and Tiger Claw won Division Two. Sea Buck, trained by Toby, was third.

*

There were five sets of colours I had always wanted to ride in – those belonging to Paul Mellon, The Queen Mother, Prince Charles, Lord Mildmay-White and Jim Joel. Ian enabled me to carry two of them; Paul Mellon's and The Queen Mother's.

Paul Mellon always had such lovely horses and he was one of the most successful owners of his era. As a little boy, I'd named one of my ponies Mill Reef, an absolute hero of mine, and I would gallop around imagining I was wearing Paul Mellon's black and gold colours.

The first time I rode for Mr Mellon was on the three-year-old Crystal Spirit. He was a brilliant bay and was so good looking. He knew it too. He felt proud, and when you sat on him it rubbed off on you.

Things couldn't have got off to a better start. We won the Freshman's Novices' Hurdle at Newbury in November 1990, by eight lengths from the David Elsworth-trained Kibreet. A month later, Jonathan Lower on Hopscotch beat us and then we made all the running to win the Silver Doctor Novices' Hurdle at Ascot. He capped that season by winning the Sun Alliance Novices' Hurdle at the Cheltenham Festival from Minorettes Girl. It crowned a wonderful 24 hours because I had won the Champion Hurdle the day before on Morley Street.

Nothing would have beaten Crystal Spirit that day. Crystal was so confident in himself and, walking around at the start having his girths done, the sun was on him and his coat looked fantastic. Having won the Champion Hurdle the day before, I felt I could fly. Throughout the race, he was always up front and jumped every hurdle immaculately. We came round the bend at the top of the hill and Brendan joined me on Upton Park. I was that relaxed and confident at the time I looked across at Brendan and said: "You're going well. You'll win," knowing all the time I had guns up my sleeves.

Turning into the home straight there was only one

barrier between victory and us, and as the hurdle came into focus, we were on the perfect stride. He lifted and jumped and then powered up the Cheltenham hill, all his muscles still strong. We passed the winning post. Although I was confident, it was wonderful to win, especially for Ian who had just lost his old school master who always liked a bet.

In October 1993, Crystal Spirit was sent chasing and he took his bow at Exeter where we were touched off by Richard Dunwoody on the Martin Pipe-trained In The Navy, despite starting at odds of 4-7. Crystal Spirit's problem was that he lacked a bit of balls. He was a lovely horse but he could be a bit windy into his fences, which was annoying because you couldn't do anything about it. At Exeter, I also think he went into the race carrying a bit too much weight, but the job was done and we were beaten.

Crystal had so much ability, but if he hadn't run for a month he would back off into the first fence and practically refuse, although, from that point, he would jump well. My biggest regret is that we should have won the Feltham at Kempton on Boxing Day, the same year.

Before the race, Ian had said: "Whatever you do, make him gallop and make it a true race." Riding around, all I could think about were Ian's instructions and I overdid it on him, and Graham Bradley on See More Indians beat us.

Ian's voice came to me again in the Sun Alliance Novices' Chase at Cheltenham in 1994. "If you are brave enough, he will be brave," he said. We were tracking Monsieur Le Cure, and Crystal was just putting down on me a bit. We were beaten going into the last but I thought I'd put Ian's theory to the test. We were still within challenging distance and Crystal always came up Cheltenham's tough hill well. I thought I had something up my sleeve.

Going to the last, for some stupid reason, I kept hearing: "If you are brave enough . . . "

So I said: "Crystal, come up." He said no, we hit the fence really hard and we struggled up the hill to finish third. It was a big race and everyone thought we should win, but I just couldn't get him into a rhythm.

Ian also trained Spinning, who should, without doubt, have won the Champion Hurdle. He was a class animal by Glint of Gold, who had been bred by Paul Mellon. He was a very special horse but he was fragile and difficult to train. He had no steering and was notoriously strong. He had to wear a drop noseband because you couldn't steer him right handed, and, after you'd ridden him, your bicep muscles would be quivering just from the sheer exertion of holding him.

He was a huge challenge and it always meant a lot to me that I rode him. Spinning gave me my most memorable ride – the kind of electrifying stuff that seldom comes in a jockey's career. It was the Cordon Bleu Handicap Hurdle at Aintree on 3 April 1993 and we had meticulously planned the race beforehand. Neale Doughty was riding Jinxy Jack, who always bolted out of the gate, so we were relying on him to make the running.

The two-mile start at Aintree is awkward because you run straight into a bend, and if you don't get a position early the other runners can block you. I was on the inner and Neale had Jinxy Jack right on the outside because he was starting to get difficult at the start. Neale's plan was to break early and come very fast into the bend. That meant I had to break fast, too, to make sure I was in front of the concertina. I did just that and got to the bend first, but there was no Jinxy Jack – he didn't get there because he didn't start.

Spinning was electric and flying. I couldn't have got him back if I'd tried, so it was a case of balance and go. At every hurdle, he was taking off a stride earlier. It was like riding a supersonic jet. We went past the grandstand and he was still locked in my hands – it took both of them to pull him around the bend. We'd taken the race by the scruff of the neck so I started to squeeze him up.

The three hurdles down the back straight are slightly wrong, and if you are going long, you really have to ask – so I did and he answered. Those were the best three hurdles I have ever met in my life. His toes had gone over the top by millimetres and he landed absolutely running. We swung into the home straight, he hit the last with his hind fetlock and flattened it, but coming down the run-in it was all over. There was no-one within breathing distance.

I eased him down past the winning-post and we glided home. We had set the course record and it still stands. That ride was so fast it was unbelievable. For me, it was my crowning moment in racing but it had taken ten years to get there.

I had a gut feeling then that it would be the last time I would ride him at Aintree and I savoured every moment for all it was worth. It was like slow motion, and as I passed the winning post I took a mental picture as if it was a freeze frame.

A month later at Haydock in the Swinton, I settled him mid-division, and he was always travelling and jumping well. We took it up three out, he popped the last and we set a new course record again – 3 minutes 33.3 seconds. That was his last ever run over hurdles and the last time I rode him. My time with Ian had run its course.

Spinning was a serious horse but he never managed to recapture that form again. He had seven more runs on the Flat and won a Conditions Stakes at Kempton in September, but then he injured himself at home and never ran again.

Ian trained a mare for the Queen Mother called Lunabelle. I felt very proud to win twice on her – at Wincanton on Boxing Day 1992 and the following September at Fontwell, where we won a novices' chase.

Towards the end of my association with the Baldings, riding for both stables probably did start to conflict, but it was at about the same time I was thinking of slowing up anyway. Maybe that is one of the reasons there has never been any hard feelings between the three of us, and we all remain very good friends.

After that ride on Crystal Spirit in the Sun Alliance, Paul Mellon wanted to put someone else up. As well as losing on the horse, they probably thought I wasn't stylish or active enough, but at least Ian broke the news to me in the proper way. He asked me into his kitchen in July and gave me a small lump of cash. It was the first present I'd ever had in all the time I had been riding for him, so I knew my time was up.

CHAPTER 13

Morley Street

At the height of my career the rewards were high. I'd be earning £6,000-8,000 a month and once, in 1991, I earned £24,000 when Morley Street won the Champion Hurdle, Crystal Spirit won the SunAlliance and I'd ridden a few others at the Festival. It was a lot of money to me. Not so long before, I'd have gone out rabbiting with my lurcher to earn enough money to buy my girlfriend a drink.

I started to get going in 1986 and my life at the top lasted six years. Being associated with the powerful yard of Toby Balding things began to slot into place in 1988. I felt a bit under pressure during those years. I had never suffered from any allergies but I used to get a very dry patch between two fingers. It would drive me mad and it didn't go until I stopped riding all those good horses. But I still enjoyed all the big races.

Most of the horses coming through were starting to make a picture so you'd know pretty well how they would run and jump and the tactical way they should be ridden. I always likened planning a ride to planning a battle. Which would be my horse's strongest weapon? Either their turn of foot or stamina, or would jumping be their forte? Then I would ride my races accordingly. I tried to keep their weak links unexposed.

Riding for Toby during his heyday is something for which I will be forever grateful. With horses like Beech Road, Kildimo, Forest Sun, Boraceva and Morley Street he had hit the ground running.

Michael Jackson's Morley Street is without doubt the best horse I have ever ridden. He was about 17hh, an easy mover, with a wonderful action. He was the perfect model of a racehorse – short coupled, lovely shoulder. Named after the London street where his owner's paper business was based, he had such high cruising gears that he could get himself out of trouble. At the peak of his career, he was unbeatable no matter who his opponents were. He had no chinks in his armour and riding him you had just two fears; being brought down or having an accident. David Elsworth had tried to buy him in 1988 and said: "Even £100,000 would not have got us around the table."

In 1989, we won the Mumm Prize Novices' Hurdle at Aintree and at the time Toby said: "I have always thought this is the best young horse I have ever had. He will start next season over hurdles to see what class he is but he is going to be some chaser – he is well-bred and very exciting. He is an absolute natural and should be unbeaten. He was very unlucky when fourth in the SunAlliance, he pulled a hurdle out of the ground and was very lame in his off-hind afterwards. I'm sure he would have won."

The following December we won the Mercury Communications Hurdle for the Sport of Kings Challenge at Cheltenham. Beech Road had already won the Waterford Crystal Champion Hurdle that year, and with Little Polveir's Grand National win, Toby was rubbing shoulders with the big boys again. But he never forgot the hard times and his feet were firmly on the ground. He must have appreciated the value of a pound because, at the same meeting, he got me to remount Going Gets Tough for second place in the Charterhouse Mercantile Leisure Novices' Chase after he failed to leave the ground at the final ditch, six from home.

The odds-on chance, French Goblin, had capsized when renewing his challenge at the second-last. Imadyna passed the post in glorious solitude, but Toby, well aware that completing would earn Going Gets Tough's owners £2,612, played the role of ramrod.

He rounded me and the horse up, and watched with great satisfaction as we jumped the remaining six obstacles to finish fully 12 minutes after Imadyna had crossed the line, but he had also had to keep the judge nailed to the floor, which probably cost him a large bottle of Scotch.

Morley Street was never stretched in the Sport of Kings Challenge, winning by seven lengths from Deep Sensation, and the press started to urge Toby to try his chance in the Champion Hurdle in 1990. Toby always felt that Beech Road was the more genuine two-miler and said: "I'm not running two in the Champion, and Morley Street has already schooled over the baby fences at home."

He felt Morley was a chaser in the making and

anyway, he had always intimated that, if he didn't go chasing, he was more likely to go for the Stayers' Hurdle rather than the Champion at the Festival. I, with the diplomacy of Henry Kissinger, told the press that I believed Morley could go to the top whatever path connections choose, although I was secretly hoping I'd get the chance to upstage Beech Road in the Champion Hurdle.

Toby ran Morley Street in the Sport of Kings Challenge at Chepstow, where we finished second, and the following year, 1990, he finally decided to run both his stars in the Champion Hurdle. Beech Road, who had always been ridden by Richard Guest, finished fourth, we were fifth and Michael Stoute's Kribensis won it.

Meanwhile, Forest Sun, a lovely chestnut horse owned by Michael Jackson, was flying. We secured our third success in just over three weeks when we landed the odds in the Baring Securities Tolworth Hurdle at Sandown.

Forest Sun's major asset was a serious turn of foot and we won again at Sandown in February before heading for the Waterford Crystal Supreme Novices' Hurdle at Cheltenham. Toby had revised plans for the gelding, who had originally been lined up to go for the SunAlliance Hurdle, preferring instead to go for the two-miler.

I had never doubted that Forest Sun had the potential to take the title because he was a real battler. It was my first Festival winner, I felt fantastic and I said afterwards: "You could throw the world at Forest Sun and he would keep running. He was on his nose at the second-last and fought like a tiger."

Morley Street kept progressing nicely and won the Sandeman Aintree Hurdle on 7 April 1990. He then had a spin in a two-mile handicap on the Flat at Goodwood in October, beating the St Leger winner Michelozzo, before we headed out to the USA to contest the Belmont Park Breeders' Cup Chase on 20 October.

*

For me, going to the States was really exciting. It was a bit like going to the fair as a kid. I loved it from the moment we met at Heathrow Airport until we returned. Any moment spent in Toby's company is always rewarding, not least setting off on a boy's own adventure to foreign lands.

I left for the States about five days before the race, travelling out with Toby and Caro Balding and their son Gerald and Michael Jackson and his wife Anita. We were stood in the queue at Heathrow Airport waiting to check in and a man standing behind offered his hand and said: "Good luck. I'm coming with you. I'm a big fan of Morley Street."

He turned out to be Johnny Egan, whose brother was head of security of all the barns at Belmont Park. He also had a niece working as a hostess on the plane and when we arrived in New York at JFK airport, she took him out through the VIP lounge.

American racing is ruled with a rod of iron, and in order to get my licence, I had to take a blood test to ensure I hadn't been taking drugs. I also had to undergo a medical examination to check I wasn't gelded. In a similar vein, Toby decided to keep me under equally firm guard and virtually kept me under lock and key until the big race was over. I was forbidden from going anywhere unless it was in a taxi in case I got mugged. I was successfully wrapped in cotton wool long enough to ensure I made it to the race, and then I was mollycoddled even further in the huge expanse of the racecourse weighing room.

When you race in America you are not allowed out of the weighing room unless it is your turn to race. The good news, however, is that, in order to prevent any boredom that might impinge upon such restrictions, there's a cinema, relaxation rooms and various other distractions. The valets look after your every need and there are even toothbrushes – everything a man could want.

Before Morley's race, I got my weight cloth ready and the guard took my saddle – you are not even allowed to touch it – and he saddles the horse. Easy life!

My biggest fear with Morley, who was the 2-1 favourite for the race, was that he was inclined to jump left. We were drawn wide on the right-hand side, and if you interfere with any other horse going into and over the first fence you are automatically disqualified. It went smoothly, he stayed straight and my biggest worry was over.

I adopted my usual waiting tactics with him, holding him up in sixth place. He jumped the portable fences well, except a slight mistake at the third-last when moving up to challenge Summer Colony, French-hope Sarh and Victorian Hill. Summer Colony had three lengths to spare over stablemate Moonstruck, who was ridden by Richard Dunwoody.

We went a good gallop all the way and I was never anxious at any moment, and as we came round the home turn I glanced at John Smart on Summer Colony and caught his attention. When he looked across, I was cheeky enough to say: "Look, this is what you call a racehorse." And there I was on the bridle.

Everybody had a shot down the back straight but I was covering them. We won by 11 lengths and it could have been more. He was the best horse I'd ridden. Forest Sun was good but Morley Street was a dream, and was the first British-trained winner of the race, which was worth $250,000.

I was full of it afterwards and said: "I saw Jimmy Lorenzo [the 1988 winner] and this horse is better than Highland Bud [the 1989 winner]. Right now he's the best hurdler in the world at this distance. He's two stones better than anyone else."

In the States you have to pay the valets there and then, including a percentage of the prize money, and I owed mine about $600 but I had no money on me...usual story. Richard Dunwoody had to find Michael Jackson who came and gave the valet a cheque, otherwise I'd still be locked in there.

*

Morley Street must have been racing's answer to Imran Khan because he was such an all-rounder. He had won on the Flat, over hurdles and over America's strange brush fences. And the wins didn't stop there.

We then ran in the Racecall Ascot Hurdle in November 1990. Mark Perrett was riding the Martin Pipe-trained Sabin Du Loir in the two-and-half-mile event and they thought they'd stretch me and go a gallop. Mark set off at a fierce pace, and as we left Swinley Bottom he was five or six lengths ahead of me. At the third-last, Morley Street jumped very fast and landed on Sabin Du Loir's heels. We came round the home turn and I had to take a pull because we would have got to the front, so we sat there waiting. It seemed like forever, but we were cruising and Sabin Du Loir was there with his ears like a little pony. However, I knew I had the world beaten so I turned to Mark and said: "Look at this Mark, we're on the bridle, you're wasting your time. You might as well go home." He was very impressive that day.

Toby had always maintained that Morley Street was a Gold Cup horse, and our chasing debut was an exercise canter in the Fred Rimell Memorial Novices' Chase at Worcester on 3 December 1990. He did nothing to disprove the claim that he was the most exciting chasing prospect in training. He was my 300th winner and he never came out of second gear. But although the world thought he was brilliant, he never felt like a natural over fences to me and I really had my doubts that he would ever make the grade because he jumped seriously left-handed and was inclined to flatten over his fences.

My theory was proved when we ran in the Feltham at Kempton on Boxing Day 1990 and it really found him out. He pulled up and Toby switched him back to hurdles. He won the Berkshire Hurdle at Newbury before we headed for the Festival and the Champion Hurdle.

We were 4-1 favourites and we moved up a gear on the final turn and, having jumped the final flight two lengths clear of Nomadic Way, we doubled that margin on the run-in. But Morley Street hated being in front, and his head went up and his stride shortened. The roar from the crowd was immense. I think every one of them must have been behind him, willing him on.

Richard Dunwoody had been hard at work on Nomadic Way between the last two flights, but he found a little more on the run-in. Morley Street had run down the last and gone to the left, but I didn't dare look over my shoulder and just kept him going to hold the chasing pair by a length.

Toby said: "Morley Street is an amazingly versatile horse. How many others could beat a St Leger winner on the Flat, fly to America and hammer them on their own patch in the Breeders' Cup Chase and return in triumph in the Champion Hurdle?" But, in typical Balding fashion, he added: "Jimmy got there too soon."

That season, he ended Desert Orchid's four-year reign as the Racegoers' Club's champion jumps racehorse and became the first hurdler to take the title since Dawn Run in 1983/84.

Morley Street was a national hero and I kept thanking my lucky stars that I was the person to be riding him, although I nearly didn't when we went back to Aintree where we played our usual starring role, winning the Sandeman Aintree Hurdle.

*

Just before the Grand National meeting, I received my first ever ban when I was found guilty of careless riding at Newton Abbot. Fortunately, the six-day suspension, which seemed pretty harsh, started just after the

National. My mount, Playpen, looked as if he hampered Born With A Veil as we turned out of the back straight in the Mile End Maiden Hurdle. The stewards reckoned that I was not far enough clear of the other horse when we drifted into the rail and, bearing in mind my experience, they said I had been "pretty careless".

I wasn't bothered about the first 'holiday' of my career and decided not to appeal. I said at the time: "I can't go against my local stewards – I've got to work with them every week. I'll just have to take my medicine." But all I had done was push out a tiring horse as I had to get after the winner. I had been riding for 19 seasons and that was my first suspension.

That day, I once again crossed swords with Ivor Lang, an old enemy from my gymkhana days, who was clerk of the course. He had described the ground as 'good to soft', which was well wide of the mark. The ground was horrible, eight horses returned lame or sore and one of the sufferers was David Barons' promising Yiragan, who I pulled up before halfway in the Plymouth Sound Radio Handicap Chase. I was tempted to say something, but decided to keep my mouth shut.

After this incident, I trekked up to Liverpool again and Morley Street won the Sandeman Hurdle for the second year running. I added another 12 bottles of port to the cellar. I've kept nearly every bottle I've won, and one day I'm planning to auction them to pay for my retirement!

Surprisingly, Morley Street was opposed in the betting that day and drifted from evens to 11-8.

Afterwards, Toby said in a defiant manner: "People seem to think my horses are over the top at this time of year, but I've proved them wrong in this race for the last two years and now we've done it again.

"Morley Street was a lot more relaxed today and was always lobbing with Jimmy, although he had to dig deep when the other horse [Nomadic Way] quickened.

"We'll try and win the Breeders' Cup Chase again and then he'll have a similar campaign to what he had this season except we'll miss the chasing bit over here!"

*

That October, we set out for the States for another go at the Breeders' Cup Steeplechase, this time with Edward Gillespie, manager of Cheltenham racecourse and organiser of the Sport of Kings Challenge, in tow. Edward had fixed us up in a bed-and-breakfast near Cheasapeake Bay. I arrived before him and, took the master bedroom, leaving him in the kids' room. Desperate to change, he used every bit of his charm to try and get me to swap. "No," I said. "I'm riding tomorrow and I need my sleep."

The people next door to the B&B had a Mustang and they offered it to Caro and Toby because we were some way out in the sticks. They let me drive that lethal contraption. As usual there was a pre-race dinner some 15 miles away and Edward and I went together, ate our meal and went to go home. We unlocked the Mustang and the alarm went off. We couldn't work out how to stop it. I said: "You drive it Edward. I can't get locked up because I've got to ride the horse tomorrow." So we drove back, alarms flashing but unnoticed by any policemen. Unbelievable.

Morley Street clocked up his second Breeders' Cup success around Fair Hill, which was a bit like a point-to-point course with a makeshift grandstand and wooden hut to change in. It was a long way from the previous season's Belmont Park luxuries, but the money was the same. That second win ensured he became a legend in his own right.

But nothing lasts forever and my relationship with Morley Street came to an abrupt conclusion after we finished no nearer than sixth in the Champion Hurdle the following year. "Nothing is so good it lasts eternally, perfect situations must go wrong," I would sing to myself because I found it so fitting at the time!

It was unfortunate that Morley Street came up against one or two problems. One is that he bled, which is when a horse's lungs haemorrhage, and I'm still certain to this day that is what happened when he flopped in the 1992 Champion Hurdle.

I had been down to Whitcombe in Dorset, where Toby was now training, to give Morley a piece of work before the race and unfortunately Toby was away. On the gallops, I jumped off, giving the horses in front a 25-yard start. Normally, half way up the gallop I'd be sitting five or ten lengths off them. We'd travel up between horses and then go on, but this day he could not get going. I had never had to ask Morley for an effort because he had always done his work cruising. There was clearly something wrong.

We got back to the stable and I have never seen a horse have such a big piddle. He must have stood there for five minutes and flooded his shavings. He then drank through his bridle for an eternity, and, by the time I had taken his tack off, he'd had another piddle, which was half as big as the first one.

His coat was dry and awful. It turned out later they'd been giving him Lasix, a diuretic that stops bleeding. The Jockey Club prohibit Lasix, and ten days before a race is about as close as you would normally administer the drug so that it doesn't show up in a dope test. Any decent judge would have spotted there was a problem with Morley Street at Cheltenham, because all the way round he was flat.

Cheltenham is quite tight and always on the turn. Down the back straight, the horse in front missed the hurdle and it bounced back up. I came to it knowing I was in serious trouble because I should not have been this far back at this stage in the race. I clawed up the inside to save every inch I could, and I thought I did well to get him up to be sixth. Royal Gait and Graham McCourt had won, about seven lengths ahead of us.

The next thing I knew I'd lost the ride. Toby told me that Michael didn't want me to ride the horse anymore. He must have decided it there and then, and he didn't even speak to me. I was devastated. We had won more money together than any other horse or rider combination. Morley Street had won 15 races from 22 starts. His earnings totalled more than £300,000.

Nikki was devastated and would have shot anyone coming within close range at that moment, but we had to accept it. Every time he raced subsequently I was wishing him to win but willing that he didn't.

Once you lose something as high profile as that, everyone else drops you as well. I felt so resentful about the fact that the horse hadn't been right, and a lot of the paddock judges had said so too. If Toby put his hand on his heart, I think he would have said the same as well. I was just the scapegoat. But the man who pays the piper calls the tune.

I told the press at the time: "A lot of friends have expressed their sympathy and support, but there are some jealous people around as well, so they hopped up and down and clapped their hands. The lads in the weighing room were up in arms but nobody's job is safe. All good things come to an end. I don't think there is a good way to end anything. I just walked away."

I received a lot of letters of support, which meant a great deal to me at the time. At least some people still had a bit of faith in me. One read: "As if Jimmy Frost hasn't lost enough of his pearly whites over the years, owner Michael Jackson certainly gave him a kick in the teeth by jocking him off both Morley Street and Forest Sun.

"After years of riding moderate horses around the country's less fashionable tracks, Frost proved himself a superb horseman when he won the Grand National on Little Polveir, and yet on Saturday he will be back where he started – at one of the gaffs.

"Frost has ridden numerous big-race victories for Michael Jackson Bloodstock Ltd, including a Champion Hurdle and two Breeders' Cup Chases and yet he was sacked for riding a so-called 'ill-judged race'.

"A possible explanation for the owner's irrational decision is that he has become so accustomed to success he has forgotten how to be gracious in defeat."

– Daniel Batty, Henley-on-Thames, Oxon.

Morley Street won at Aintree with Richard Dunwoody on board, by which time I had stopped thinking and hit a bit of a depression. With hindsight, I was making a big mistake. He was in the Martell Aintree Hurdle and Minorettes Girl was in the same race. The year before, in the SunAlliance Novices' Hurdle at Cheltenham, I'd beaten her on Crystal Spirit so I knew her pretty well. I should have rung Paddy Mullins and asked if I could ride her because I knew we could have beaten Morley Street.

I had the perfect plan for the race and would have known how to fight the battle because I knew Morley Street's weak link, which I kept to myself for many years. Minorettes Girl always went off some 20 lengths clear but Morley Street had to expose himself at some stage during the race and come out into the open. I'd have almost stopped Minorettes Girl going into the second-last, let Morley go in front again and then I'd have kept on his tail and half way up the run-in we'd have gone on again. I didn't think of this until a week later and regret not phoning her trainer. As it was, Morley Street beat her half a length.

Cool Ground had come spare in the Grand National and Toby tried to get me back on him, but I'd ridden him in the Irish National and in a chase at Newcastle and each time he'd hit a brick wall. I was certain he wouldn't stay the full four miles so I said no. He finished tenth to Party Politics. I was still feeling gutted but I would rather have been at Hereford than trailing around at the back in the Grand National. I said at the time: "I have been riding for 20 years now and I'm nearly 34. I've been incredibly lucky with injuries.

"I'm still getting plenty of rides and its winners that pay the bills – I don't mind if it's a seller at Taunton. Whilst the rest are going to Liverpool I plan to ride Auction Law for David Barons at Hereford."

Morley Street won the Coral Elite Hurdle at Cheltenham in November, again with Dunwoody riding him, then went for the Racecall Ascot Hurdle five days later. One kind supporter called David Cotterill from East Sussex wrote: "There is little doubt that Morley Street is back to his form of two years ago. There is also little doubt that he really should have won the Racecall Hurdle at Ascot last Friday.

"It would be fair to say that the eight-year-old fooled Richard Dunwoody into believing that he would surely see the race through, but Muse wasn't stopping and surely Morley Street could have been held up a little longer? The fact that he only got beaten a short head gives no consolation to those who had their fingers burned.

"I would love to know what was going through Jimmy Frost's mind during the debacle. He was made the scapegoat for last season's Champion Hurdle failure.

"The trainer has since stated openly that he was never totally happy with the gelding last season, and in the light of events at Ascot it furthers the absurdity of Frost's sacking.

"I believe it is time for the owner, Mr Jackson, to eat a large slice of humble pie and return the ride to the pilot who knows the horse best, namely one J. Frost."

If I had been an eagle I would not have missed

Michael Jackson's bald head. Until he jocked me off, he had been very good to me and he was after, but I could not believe he could blow like that. He had always been very fair and I can appreciate it all went wrong for him in the Champion Hurdle. If it had been the horse just feeling off colour it would have been hard enough to accept, but I'm convinced he thinks I stopped the horse.

I did lose a lot of rides as a result. One minute I was big in fashion, the next I wasn't and in the fickle world of racing you are soon forgotten. My family have always been incredibly supportive and Nikki always takes the brunt of my disappointment but when the children smile, they bring you around much quicker. At the end of the day, yes, I'd been sacked, but my family were all healthy, we have a great life and there are more important things to worry about than a horserace.

During the bad times my natural instinct is to be alone. I don't want anyone around me and I just want to get somewhere I can't see anyone and the phone doesn't ring. Since I was 14 years old this is always how I've coped. I'll grab a horse and go for a gallop on the moors and that's what I did. Other than losing Combermere, it is one of the lowest points I have ever reached during my race-riding career.

Toby Balding was as supportive as he could be, and when he asked me to ride Morley Street for him again, I was in the car driving to Exeter. My initial reaction was, "I can't do that. It would be like putting Prince Charles and Diana back together again."

He said: "Don't be so bloody stupid. You are a

professional."

So I did ride Morley Street in the Tripleprint Gold Cup Handicap Chase at Cheltenham in 1993 and we trailed around and finished seventh. He was a shadow of his former self and it was sad to remember him that way. He raced another eight times but never won again and was retired in 1995.

*

With the benefit of hindsight, I realise how lucky I was to be riding for Toby and his brother Ian because I was never really that ambitious as a jockey, and anyway, my aim had always been to train horses. Without them I would never have tasted big-race glory. I was happy at home and never tempted to move away; although spending hours behind the wheel of a car – I did 80,000 miles one year – when there were 101 other things to do, was one of the worst parts of the job.

Although I was jocked off Morley Street, I never felt any resentment towards Toby. He was a serious mentor for me and I never once regretted my association with him. His friendship is one I will always value and at least I repaid his faith in me with some good wins. They are golden memories.

CHAPTER 14

Life Moves On

I had a gut feeling that Peter Bolton was winding up Michael Jackson over the riding of his horses, which had a detrimental effect on our relationship. I had ridden Cool Ground for Bolton, and in 1991 I had deputised for the injured Luke Harvey and won the Jim Ford at Wincanton when he was trained by Reg Akehurst. Toby said to me after that win: "Jim, you are actually beginning to look quite stylish." But the horse was a very good ride.

Luke then finished fourth to Garrison Savannah in the Gold Cup; then I rode him in the Irish Grand National on 1 April and finished third. Omerta won it for Martin Pipe, ridden by the young amateur Adrian Maguire.

Peter Bolton never explained why he had changed jockeys for the Irish National. Perhaps Luke knows why he lost the ride, or perhaps it was a natural prelude to the following season's arrangements when Toby took over from Akehurst at Bolton's lavish Whitcombe Manor training operation in Dorset.

I rode Cool Ground again in the Warwick National Trial on 18 January 1992 and we finished second to Woodgate. Next stop was the Tote Eider Chase at Newcastle. I never believed Cool Ground would stay four miles, although everybody else must have done because he started the 5-2 favourite. He jumped really well and, six out, we were in the lead. Three out we were headed and then he ran out of petrol, as he did in the Irish National, when we blundered two fences from home. Bolton felt he should have won and blamed me. That was the end of another relationship, which made the atmosphere at Whitcombe tense. I stopped enjoying going down there. It became a job and not a pleasure.

At the time, Bolton had a lovely grey mare called Absalom's Lady and together we won a novices' hurdle at Fontwell very easily on 12 December 1991. When Bolton jocked me off for the ride I gave Cool Ground in the Eider, he said to me: "You were always more interested in Absalom's Lady than Cool Ground." As if that made it all right. She went on to win ten races in total and became a real star for David Elsworth, who took over at Whitcombe after Toby. Her wins included the BonusPrint Christmas Hurdle at Kempton on Boxing Day in 1994 with Paul Holley on board, and the William Hill Haldon Gold Cup Chase at Exeter in 1996, when she was trained by Gay Kelleway.

Being jocked off horses is all part and parcel of being a jockey. One minute you are the flavour of the month and the next you are kicked into touch with the rest of them.

I lost the rides on those wonderful horses, but I gained a few as well, although being legged up on the

David Barons-trained Rocktor did my career more harm than good. Since I first turned professional, David Barons had always been very good in supporting me right up until he finally retired in 1994, with nearly 1,000 winners under his belt. I'd regularly go down to his yard at Morleigh, in south Devon, for schooling sessions, during which Mr Barons could get very wound up. The pace of life was pretty vigorous down there and I always felt under a lot of pressure riding for him, but he got results and I was glad to be part of it. It worked well, with his wife Jeni Renfree training the horses, whilst he acted as the front man with the owners.

I'd school the youngsters, and part of their initial training was to jump a line of logs that were fenced in down a jumping lane. If your horse stopped, there was nowhere to go, which would wind up Mr Barons even more, as he would have to dismantle the fencing to get the horse out. There would be a lot of swearing and he'd shout: "This is not a perfect world and we have not got time to be out here all day." Every moment was precious to him and it's no wonder he was such a successful businessman.

But he stuck by me and one horse I loved riding for him was Topsham Bay, who belonged to Sir Eric Parker. We still hold the course record at Newbury after we won the Paul Croucher Memorial Trophy Handicap Chase on 26 March 1993, which is remarkable because it was only a two-horse race. Jimmy McCarthy was still claiming five pounds and was on the Oliver Sherwood-trained Royle Speedmaster who had 9st 9lbs on his back.

Sherwood wanted to gallop my horse into the ground and make the weight tell because Topsham Bay was carrying 12st. Jimmy rode as if he had the devil up his backside, but Topsham Bay was excellent and jumped brilliantly. Fence after fence he made up ground and he jumped the last spring-heeled and we won, which was a poignant moment because Paul Croucher, who was killed in a car crash, had been a good friend of mine.

Rocktor was a different kettle of fish to Topsham Bay, and when Nigel Hawke was taken off, I took over. Rocktor was a very difficult horse, and at ditches he tended to leave his hind legs behind. It became a bit of a mental thing with him because you knew he would deck out. He was also very lazy.

I rode him in the Mitsubishi Shogun Golden Miller Trophy Handicap Chase at Cheltenham on 21 April 1993 and, after some pretty horrendous blunders, he eventually got rid of me at the 17th fence. I was knocked unconscious, stood down for a week and missed winning the Whitbread at Sandown on Topsham Bay. So much for getting the rides on other jockeys' horses.

The following year, I was looking forward to riding Topsham Bay in the Grand National. We looked to have a very good chance, however the ground came up heavy, which went against him. He raced up with the leaders until we were badly hampered at the 13th and I came off.

He then ran in the Whitbread on 23 April 1994, but the ground was very fast and it was telling on the horse. He jumped well, but he was never fast enough to get into the race and he was heavily beaten going into the railway fences. I kept him going to see if we could sneak some prize money but he had nothing left and Mr Barons accused me of not giving him a ride. I obviously wasn't hard enough on horses for Mr Barons' liking.

*

In racing as in life, when it rains it pours and – not for the first time – I found myself on the receiving end of a lot of criticism. After a period of despondency, when I could quite easily have chucked it all in, given my age as well, I had a long hard think about my career. I realised that what I really enjoyed was training and race riding, particularly progressing youngsters through the ranks, so together with my family I made a conscious decision that this was where my future lay. I have never looked back.

But that is not to say I still didn't lose some pretty good rides, although this time it was through sheer bad luck. Walter Dennis, who trains on the north Cornwall coast near Bude, had a lovely horse called Coome Hill on whom I'd won the Badger Beer Handicap Chase on 9 November 1996 at Wincanton. He'd won it very easily and was a serious contender for the Hennessy Cognac Gold Cup three weeks later at Newbury, his next engagement. Needless to say, I was really looking forward to the ride.

At home, we trained a young horse called Bishop's Castle and I rode him in a two-mile novice chase at Hereford on 20 November 1996 and fell. I'd got away with the whole field avoiding me until Jacqui Oliver, riding King's Shilling, galloped right over the top of me. She can't have seen me.

As I hit the ground, I knew there was a big field behind me. I curled up very tight and prayed that everyone would avoid me. As silence started to reign and I thought the field has passed with no more than a bump or two, suddenly it felt like I'd been hit by an Exocet missile, which picked me up and carried me across the ground. I was tangled amongst the hind legs of a horse. When I finally came to rest, I knew I was badly hurt. I could get no air. My eyes focused on the blue sky. I was on my back looking upwards. Still no air.

I was lying there thinking "I don't want to die at the back of an open ditch in Hereford," because I knew by now that I was pretty seriously injured. The first-aid man arrived and I could hear his words as he asked me what piece of me hurt. I couldn't answer him because I still couldn't get any air. Again I kept telling myself I must relax and I kept thinking: "How long can I last with no air?"

I managed to get a small breath and the ambulance came and took me to Hereford General where it was diagnosed I had broken seven ribs and punctured a lung. I spent a week in hospital. Jamie Osborne picked up the ride on Coome Hill, who went on to win the Hennessy. That was probably one of the hardest races to miss, as I knew there wouldn't be many more chances of winning a decent prize.

You always think falling off hurts more when you get older, but it hurts just as much when you are young. I'd always been very lucky with injuries but I have always kept very fit and supple and, when I was younger, I did a lot of floor work like trunk curls and stretches and I used to be able to sit with my forehead on the floor. I'm sure that my fitness and flexibility has helped me keep in one piece.

When I was an amateur, I did a lot of running between rides, two miles around the block, getting quicker every time. I also used to swim every Monday; I'd do a length under and 50 lengths on top. Rides were fairly spaced out, but when I was riding point-to-point, I was probably more dedicated to fitness. I was very hard on myself and, when I progressed to riding as a professional, the foundations were laid.

Now that I've hung up my boots after 30 years in the saddle, I'm really proud to look back on my medical book. When I was 16, I'd had plenty of falls off the ponies but I'd never broken anything. I'd been getting a few rides under Rules and a local paper ran an article entitled "Jockey in the Making". It said: "And there's still one hurdle – this one a dangerous one. Jimmy has fallen many times – but never broken anything. In the tough profession of the National Hunt world, a busted collarbone keeps a rider out of racing just ten days. But something more serious could happen, which even if it didn't jar Jimmy's courage, could prove extremely damaging. 'Out of sight out of mind,' as Billy Williams said, recalling a good professional lightweight jockey who was laid up for several months after a bad road accident and the many miles he'd happily drive just for one ride on one of Billy's horses. The Sport of Kings may look good through the bottom of a winning owner's champagne glass, but for the 200 or so National Hunt riders, it's an endless gruelling course."

It's a good job I couldn't read because looking at that now, it could have put me off for life. And the journalist's predictions proved unfounded. During my riding career, I never did break my collarbone and my medical book has just 15 red entries, which is when the doctor declares you unfit to ride through injury. I have a tremendous sense of self-preservation. The book was issued on 28 July 1974, and my first accident was 12 years later off Stars and Stripes, when I broke a few ribs.

That season, I also came off Kingswood Kitchens, who fell at the third-last at Stratford, which is on the other side of the course to the medical room. The first thing I remember was the last of six stitches in my forehead with no anaesthetic. Thank goodness for Paul Barton and his good judgement on that occasion. I had concussion and was not fit to drive, despite the fact that the doctors passed me fit. Thankfully, Paul refused to let me drive home.

I was stood down on a further five occasions with concussion and, when I first rode for John Blake, I fell off Mr Playfull at Newton Abbot in 1997. I was pretty knocked about but still managed to get to Powderham Castle that night to watch Chris de Burgh, a surprise birthday present from Nikki.

The medical book can work in your favour as well. In my second-to-last season, I got myself signed off with stiff hands for a few days on a cold damp March day at Exeter – I didn't feel like riding! My last injury was on 1 November 2001, when I came off Defendtherealm at Exeter and had concussion. The last couple of years I was riding, I definitely got a bit tired, but then I was the old man of the changing room and not even Peter Pan could ride National Hunt horses forever.

CHAPTER **15**

A New Lease Of Life

You never get to paradise, although it is an interesting path trying to get there, and riding brilliant horses like Spinning, Morley Street and Crystal Spirit is as good as it gets for a jockey. But nothing lasts forever. I wasn't getting any younger and decent lads like Adrian Maguire were coming along. When I started to lose the good rides, my confidence took a nosedive and I went through a difficult period for about six months. I'd feel okay about my riding one minute and the next I was questioning every aspect of it. I really felt like I had lost the edge.

Then one day, I gave myself a really good talking to: "Frosty," I said, "either you quit riding now or you get on with it. You can't go back to being 25 and riding horses like Morley Street again, but there are a lot of nice young horses, which need teaching their job, and there's plenty of racing to be done. You know you can do it."

When you become wrapped up in your own feelings

of self-doubt and self-pity, it is easy to forget what is around you and to lose sight of what you really want. Training had always been first and foremost in my mind; and we had a nice lot of young horses at the yard, fantastic owners, who have always been very supportive, and a brilliant team. So, from the early 1990s, I enjoyed a new lease of life. There was a renewed bounce in my stride, and I got down to the job of enjoying my racing and training.

However, there will always be a few little low points, like when I was finally served with my first ban, after 19 seasons riding. It irks me now that the source of my troubles and subsequent fines has been Newton Abbot, my local track where many of the friends with whom I grew up are stewards.

There are times when you like to think you have got everything just right for a race and you fancy your chances strongly, but things don't always go to plan and, much as you'd like to beat the bookies, horses are not machines. They are living, breathing creatures and they can't be turned on or off like a car. There are too many imponderables for plans to always work.

I've been 'done' twice for schooling in public, most recently at Newton Abbot on 16 July 2001. Kitley Creek, who belonged to stable stalwart Mrs Josie Bastard, was a very difficult horse. He was a very anxious type who would even lose control of his senses at home if something upset him. That day at the races completely blew his mind. Going down to the start in the Newton Abbot Novices' Hurdle, I felt like I had no steering and I couldn't go left or right. He wouldn't even stand still enough for the starter's assistant to tighten his girth, and, at one stage, I wanted to get off and lead him back home because he was hard to hold at the walk and he was sweating badly, which is a sign of fear.

When we passed the water jump he had mentally left me. The race had really distressed him. I asked for an effort, he changed his legs twice but was going nowhere, so I collected him up together, rode him into the bridle and finished fifth. I wanted to get him home safely so that the experience would not leave him traumatised. The stewards did not see it that way. It cost us £1,500 in fines altogether, I was banned for five days, and the horse was banned for a month.

We then ran him a month later at Exeter and this time I rode him differently and rode out as the stewards wanted. I jumped him out the gate handyish and he had nothing on the home turn. I pulled my whip and cracked him a couple of times so the stewards could see. There was no response. I drove him with hands and heels up the home straight, just so that they could see I was making the horse finish. After the race, he was very distressed and took a while to recover. That poor horse had a horrible experience, yet I had ridden it how the stewards wanted. That's not putting the horse's welfare first. It's about time stewards started to look long and hard at some of their decisions.

I've since sold him to trainer Martin Hill, who has put a mirror in his stable to try and help him cope with life a bit better – mirrors are supposed to help some horses. But that horse could not cope with racing. Some of the stewards' decisions should be reversible with hindsight because it affects your reputation and it can also cost you a lot of money. I believe I had done a very good piece of riding, getting him settled enough, and nursing him round to get him home so that he would not be left with horrible memories. Horses can't look forward, they can only remember what has happened to them in the past, and that horse did not deserve to be hit all along the run-in, especially as he was not even placed.

Mrs Bastard has bred her own racehorses for years on the Kitley Estate near Yealmpton in south Devon. She is a huge supporter of racing and the type of person that is the backbone of the sport. She did not deserve that treatment.

Decisions like that make you feel very sore and I do believe the stewards go through phases of picking on people. It's as if a jockey or trainer gets in trouble at one meeting and the rest of the stewards around the country jump on the bandwagon. A lot of stewards have no practical riding experience, but I don't think that really matters because you can still be a good teacher and a good observer without being able to do it yourself.

My biggest gripe is the inconsistencies in their decisions. Jockeys like me and Richard Guest are able to get the best out of horses without ever looking as if we are really riding them. I would class myself as one of the best men in England for schooling horses. It's all about rhythm, confidence, patience and practice. The horse has got to be happy and he has got to want to do it.

I rode a horse at Exeter once and she jarred her tendons, which I could feel during the race, and I was expected to ride her out. I was fined under the non-triers' rule and the next day had a vet's certificate stating her problem. I was going to appeal but the years have taught me to sit back and accept the punishment. I like to think its out of a sense of courtesy and the wish to avoid a scene, but it's more likely to be the fact that my fine was £120 and, by the time I had taken a day off work, bought a ticket to London and paid a solicitor to represent me, it just wasn't worth it.

*

At Hawson Court, we had plenty going on. We moved into our new house in 1992, and the donkeys and cattle, as well as the horses, continued to play a huge part in the family's life. The donkeys also helped Daniel and Hadden learn the serious business of betting. God help the racing world if they end up making their careers in it!

From the late 1960s, my father kept a team of donkeys which were contracted to Pontins, who ran a holiday park in Torquay. Every Tuesday and Thursday morning, we took the donkeys to Pontins for the children to ride them in derbys. Eventually, Pontins was sold for development and so we let the team go to some people in Exeter. We went for several years without any donkeys, until a holiday company rang and asked if we would do the rides for them. At first I said no, then I thought about the financial implications, decided it was worth it and, in 1985, set about collecting a team of donkeys, some from as far afield as Ireland.

In those days, there wasn't any summer Jump racing, so it worked very well. The donkeys lived as a herd and we did a lot of fetes and open days at racing yards. It was good fun watching people like Adrian Maguire getting bucked off one minute, only to see that same donkey walking sedately around the ground with a child on board.

Having the donkeys was great because it meant we spent a lot of time together as a family, going to various different functions. The boys liked it in particular, as they started to make a lot of money at the derbys. Daniel would back Hadden to win on the Tote but, of course, people soon cottoned on that it was the donkey man's son who was winning all the races. So Hadden would get himself beaten a couple of times, until Daniel had his money on again, and Hadden would grab his fast donkey, Baby Blue, and they'd clean up again on another race. They had it well sussed and Daniel is quite a little punter. It will be interesting to see what happens if Hadden does pursue his dream and become a jockey! Daniel could end up quite rich.

Eventually, we sold the team in 1999, when summer Jump racing began to take over. We were getting really busy and had to ask someone else to help us with the donkeys. However, when we discovered the arrangement wasn't working, we let them go to Julie Wyborough in Brixham and they still work as a team on Paignton seafront. It was sad to see those old faces go. They'd been around for so many years, had taught the children to ride and had been a huge part of our lives.

Summers were also spent travelling to the agricultural shows with the Charolais cows. Every year, Nikki, the children, our head lad Derek McKenna and one of our pure-bred Charolais cows stay at Paul Tylor's farm on the Lizard. We'll show the cow at Stithians and Liskeard Show and take in a little holiday at the same time, although, with the predominance of summer racing and the children's own competitive careers, it is getting more difficult now.

I've built up a nice little pedigree herd, purely as a result of winning the Grand National. After I won the race Ted Harvey, Little Polveir's owner, asked what I would like as a present. He wouldn't give me any money, but wanted to give me a gift. Daniel was 18 months old so an exotic holiday was out of the question, and, anyway, at the end of it, all you have is a photograph album and a few memories. An antique or a painting would be nice, but you would never sell either, so there was not much point in that, and most houses are broken into at some stage so both would be vulnerable.

However, I'd always liked cattle. If you lost me at county shows I'd be in the cattle shed going up and down the lines admiring the different breeds. I'd just bought myself a couple of Charolais and I thought I didn't have enough money and I was probably too tight anyway to pay for a decent one. So I rang Ted and asked if he would buy me a couple of foundation cows and he agreed. I went to local breeders Richard and Sue Northmore near Plymouth and picked out two called Lovaton Vogue and Lovaton Coombe, and from them I built up the herd. From Lovaton Coombe we bred Frostys Lynx and she is one of the top cows in the country. She weighs about a ton.

Derek and I have had some great times going to the cattle shows. They involve a whole different set of people. We first showed a cow called Lovaton Elude. She was three years old before she went to her first show, so she took a bit of breaking and teaching to load. We had just laid the lawn at our new home, Holybrook, and we didn't have a flat place to load her. Having nearly a ton of cow running around on the end of a rope is harder than trying to get an unbroken four-year-old horse into a lorry.

There is an awful lot to showing cattle and we've picked up a lot of tips over the years. You have to soap the Charolais up and then backcomb her hair to make her all fluffy. Then you trim the tummy line and curl the coat on her neck to make her look taller. Derek and I are really quite good with our hairdressing skills on our blonde beauties. We take our cow along, pamper her to pieces, and promote the breed locally at the same time. The farmers take the mickey out of us because they know really we are horse people. "You won't get that bugger to jump, Frosty!" or "You won't win no races with that one, lad!" they shout.

Being a rural lad from a farming world, it's great to be involved in a different aspect of Westcountry life. Of course it's as corrupt as any type of showing. A friend once told me that he had two cows to show. He showed one, and a pretty young girl showed the other. He was about fifth or sixth in the line and she won it and then they went in another class, swapped cows, and she still won.

Farming is changing and we have cut down on the number of cattle we keep on our land. Over the course of the next few years, Holybrook, which is just a mile down the road from Hawson Court, will be the new training centre for the racehorses so they will take over from the cattle. We will always have a few so that we can rotate the grazing, and the plan is to reduce quantity and increase quality.

The children also take up a lot of our time. My parents spent a lot of time with me and, as you grow older, you realise how precious that time is. My children are great fun; and they cost us a fortune, but I'm very pleased to be able to spend the moments I have with them. Of course I'm hoping that one day they might be able to repay me!

Daniel wants to go into racecourse management; Hadden wants to ride – he is very talented, intensely competitive and far better than I ever was as a child; and Bryony's too young to know yet, but her showing career is really taking off and she loves riding her ponies.

The kids take a great interest in the racing and will ride out at weekends. Some children grow up feeling second to the business but mine are my priority. If someone can't get me on the telephone because I'm with the kids and subsequently complains, I'll suggest they find someone else to train their horses.

I go showjumping with Hadden most weekends and it's like growing up all over again. We go to the shows, and the girls I was competing against when I was a child are now holding their children's ponies. When I was 14 or 15 and first started going out in Torquay, dad was always there to drop us off or pick us up. I was so lucky and I want to do that for my children.

*

During the last ten years I was riding, there were no great stars and winning the Badger Beer at Wincanton on Coome Hill on 19 November 1996 was my last big winner. But riding a four-timer at Newton Abbot on 18 March 1998 was brilliant and equalled those big-race successes. There was still life in the old dog!

It was the Wednesday of the Cheltenham Festival. We took two home-breds to the track and two we'd bought the same day at Newmarket Sales. We knew all four were fit and well and in their right race, but you never think all will win. If you win with one you're happy. The first horse into the winner's enclosure was Blue Blazer. He was bought out of Ben Hanbury's stable at Newmarket for about 1,000 guineas and he'd won five races on the Flat.

I asked the lad who was leading him: "Is he a complete crock?" He said "No," but he believed he had cracked his cannon bone. He came home and his joints were showing a bit of wear. I rang Ben Hanbury, told him I'd bought the horse, and he told me not to canter him because his joints wouldn't stand it and that his American owners would like him back if we wanted to get rid of him. I thought that was really odd. They'd sent a horse to Newmarket where they were basically chucking him to the wolves, and yet they said they would have him back.

He was a very pretty horse and Nikki was thinking of showing him, so she rode and schooled him and did a bit of flat work with him at home before he eventually went back up to the yard and started to do a few canters. One day he pulled up very lame halfway through his work.

I thought: "Oh dear, we've found the problem."

I checked him all over and he was hitting the

sesamoid bone in his leg quite badly. I gave him a few days off and then kept him in boots forever after that. He went back into work and then started running in the Moonlight Steeplechases, which local hunts run over the summer months to raise funds. We always take the horses in support and Brendan Powell came down for a charity race. Blue Blazer did that and loved it, so we decided to try him under Rules and he won two or three for us including on four-timer day. When he began to lose a bit of form and his joints started to play up we gave him to Ursula Hambley who worked for us all those years ago. He lives in Cornwall now and she rides him on Par beach every morning.

Hold Your Ranks then won the Horses For Courses 2m 5f handicap chase. He was a bit of a specialist on the Newton Abbot course, and he was our first home-bred winner of the day. We were pretty much tailed off with a circuit to run and a full 25 lengths down, and then he just picked up and started to run about a mile from home. The others had gone too fast and were starting to stop, and, from the water, which is the third-last, he was flying. We had taken it up before the last and I held my breath over the final fence because he wasn't very brave in front, but he jumped that well, so that was two in the bag. That was his sixth win at the course. He never managed to win anywhere else, and he ended his career on a high note when he won a selling handicap chase on 3 November 1999.

A double was a good day for us, whatever happened to the other horses. Then Defendtherealm was in the Little Close Handicap Hurdle over 2m 5f. I didn't really think he would win because he had missed some work and was a bit podgy, and he did finish a tired horse. However, I kept him going using hands and heels to keep him committed. He was out of Armagnac Princess, the mare who had really got me going.

Then we came to Mr Jack's little horse, Mystic Hill, a beautifully-bred horse, by Shirley Heights out of a Nureyev mare who was bought out of Newmarket. He had some good Flat form and Amanda Perrett had recommended him. He was a fine little hurdler, although when he first went schooling, he approached the fence like he knew what he was doing and then ducked out rapidly to the left, galloping across the field as if he was expecting a good hiding. He had obviously been hit and was more afraid of the hiding he was going to get than jumping the fences. It took a while to get his confidence back. He didn't have a problem with his jumping, he was just worried about it.

He was in the Jokers Handicap Hurdle over two miles and he was always travelling well. As we came past the water, he was full of running, quickened up on the home straight and sprinted clear. Mr Jack said: "Well done, but why did you have to win by 20 lengths!" I said: "I just got too excited!"

The locals were fantastic and Newton Abbot is brilliant for me. The atmosphere is superb, with all my friends there, and the crowd was really cheering me on. So that was the four-timer. I've only had the one! The letters of congratulations were fantastic and Martin Pipe's letter is still on the office wall. I found it very touching that he should take time out to write a letter to me.

*

When the pressure eased off, after I stopped riding the big horses, I found my services were in demand to help budding young jockeys learn how to school over fences. In 1992, David Pipe, son of the champion trainer Martin, came to Hawson Court to learn how to jump. Martin had asked me at the races and I was pleased to do it. I just hoped I'd make a good job of it.

We'd just built the house, there was no furniture and David was our first guest. He was 18 years old and his primary objective was to beat his dad, who had ridden one point-to-point winner. "You've got to get me to do that," he said.

He'd spent time with Criquette Head in France and Michael Dickinson in America, so I thought he must know a bit. "How much jumping have you done?" I asked.

"None," he replied. I thought he was trying to make sure he started on the bottom rung of the ladder, but I was sure he must have jumped before. "Surely he couldn't be Martin Pipe's son and not know how to ride?" I thought.

We had a chaser called Torre Trader, who won a couple of handicap chases, and had been consistently placed. He was a lovely horse who had had an early education showjumping, and in 28 runs he'd fallen twice and unseated twice. So I thought he would be the ideal horse for David to start on.

We went out into the field, where we have jumps at two and three feet, and I thought: "He's got to be able to do that." The horse started to refuse to jump and it slowly dawned on me that David had been telling the truth. He really hadn't left the ground on a horse before and Torre Trade had no idea what he was asking him to do.

I rode over on my horse: "I think we had better start at the beginning – you are telling the truth," I said.

We went back into the school and I put him on the lunge on Nikki's lovely big cob, Jones. We progressed to ground poles and cavaletti and, by the end of the week, he was going over the logs. By the time he went home, he was jumping fences.

Jones was a show cob with a hogged mane that can make life difficult for a novice with nothing to hang on to. But, intent on my mission of turning this 6'4" lad into a jockey, I got carried away. "No, no, do it again. Not like this, like that," I would bellow as he went round and round on this cob with no saddle and nothing to hold on to.

David couldn't walk for three days after that but he would not give in. That just shows what he's made of, because he stuck to it. His ability to absorb information and learn is endless and he'll make a terrific trainer when he eventually takes over from his dad.

We had a lovely time and, everywhere I went, David came too. It was amusing if the Pipes and the Frosts had runners at the same meeting. There would be my mum and David with the owners in one little group, and Martin Pipe, Carol and all their gang in another cluster. People must have wondered what was going on.

When David rode his winner at Cheltenham I felt very proud to have been part of his education. He was very, very good, it's just such a pity he's so tall because he could have gone far as an amateur. I have been lucky enough to have ridden for Martin Pipe right from the start and there is nothing better than being asked to ride a nice horse that you know will have been schooled well. The first horse I rode for him was The Burghermeister at Taunton in an amateurs' race and we finished third and I kept up my association until 2002, when I rode Potentate at Chepstow.

When I first rode for Martin, he had started to train horses in a completely different way and he was breaking new ground. His horses were fitter, they looked better and they were delivering the results. But success in Britain breeds contempt. For some reason, it is within our nature to feel jealousy towards achievement instead of celebrating it as something positive.

Martin has had more than his fair share of bad press and there are some journalists who have a lot to answer for. There is something in the British attitude that dictates that as soon as anyone is at the top of their game, they have to be knocked back down again. I really cannot fathom out why people want to berate success, other than that they succumb to jealousy. I suppose we are all guilty of that at some stage or another, but not to the extent where people go out of their way to make unproven accusations against a trainer just because he happens to have found the key to getting the best from his horses.

I have known Martin for many years and I have nothing but respect for him. His achievements are outstanding and, every time he trains another winner, I think: "Good on you Martin," because he is a genius, certainly of this generation, and I genuinely feel very proud to have been associated with him. Someone once said to me that if you only trained one winner, you would have more friends than enemies; train any more than that, and you'll have more enemies than friends. I experienced it often enough when I was perpetually accused of being a cheat on the gymkhana circuit. But, before I started winning, I would look at the other children, see what they were doing and then go home and practise continually until I started to beat them.

Martin continually seeks advice from so many different places, not just from the equestrian world, and it is something everyone in racing can learn from. He plans his races meticulously. He is not scared to try out new methods; he still does and that is why he remains ahead of the game.

*

Anyway, off my soap box and back onto racing. In June 1998, I rode a double at Newton Abbot including Jimmy's Cross, my last ever winner for Toby Balding. Since I first won on Lucky Vane for him in 1987, I'd ridden a winner every year, except 1997. Jimmy's Cross was a bit of a monkey and had to be covered up and kept on the inside rail. We just got up on the line to win the Come Summer Racing Novices Chase. I also won for Mr Jack that day on Mystic Hill. I put up a pound overweight in the handicap hurdle and he won by 28 lengths.

We have always done well at Newton Abbot and have turned over a few hotpots in our time. On 3 February 1999, the Venetia Williams-trained Silk Vestments was 6-4 on for the Banana Boat Novices' Hurdle but finished third behind our own Mr Perfecta. Liz Vince, who has been with us for many years, looked after the horse and it was nice for her because she was responsible for the mating of Dona Perfecta with Mr Tyler's stallion Landyap.

After I rode my 500th winner, Newton Abbot staged the Jimmy Frost 500 Not Out Handicap Chase on 29 June 2001. Unfortunately we didn't manage to win. Our own stallion Morpeth, by Sadler's Wells out of a mare by Blakeney, who was unable to race because of bad joints, has also been making his mark and on 11 November 2001 at Exeter he had his first winner when Baloo won the novices' hurdle.

We churned out the winners with regularity over the years, but as my years advanced, I began to feel a bit of pressure about retiring, not because my time was up, but because people constantly questioned me about when I was finally going to hang up my boots.

Life at Hawson Court was rattling along at a fair old pace and Holybrook was beginning to resemble a madhouse with a constant stream of visitors, guests, dogs, cats, ponies, horses, children and orphaned chickens and ducks arriving, which Daniel took great delight in looking after. That almost surreal atmosphere of happiness, which had pervaded since I was a child, was still there and life really was great.

However, things changed very suddenly one terrible autumn day and Hawson Court lost its innocence forever.

CHAPTER 16

A Sad Day

Disgust, disbelief, shock, outrage, sadness . . . nothing can describe how we felt when we discovered Jessie Hurlestone had been murdered in her caravan behind the stables at Hawson Court.

Our life came to a grinding halt that autumn day. With hindsight I could have stopped it. I knew Stephen Webber was getting stressed, but I didn't realise how bad it was. I'd seen him once or twice lurking around the yard and he said he'd lost his dog. He'd broken down at the kitchen table a couple of times saying he loved Jessie. He said he didn't mind if there was no sex in the relationship, as long as she was loyal and appreciated him. I told him girls weren't like that, and that she was bound to go off with someone eventually. He said he wouldn't be able to stand that and he'd kill her if she did.

Derek and I had been riding down the road together and Jessie was in front. As we rode along he related an incident to me that he had seen earlier that day. Stephen had had a fit at the yard and Derek found him lying on the ground. He was moaning about Jessie and how much he loved her. Derek told him to grow up and move on. I said to Derek I wouldn't be surprised if he took a 12-bore to himself and Jessie, and I meant it. Although Stephen had been a lifelong friend, there was always a nagging doubt about his mental state, particularly when he was depressed.

He didn't take a gun, but instead used an iron hook and bludgeoned her to death with 30 blows, beating her head to a pulp as she lay in her bed in her caravan at Hawson Court on 20 October 1995.

*

Jessie had come to work for us after being recommended by Sarah Williams, who trains in north Devon. She came from Romford, Essex, from a very unhorsey family. Both her parents were teachers and her father was into politics. He was an active member of the Liberal Democrat party.

Jessie was devoted to the horses and she was in her element at Hawson. She had found a job that for her was paradise on earth. She lived for horses and almost as soon as she could walk, she started taking riding lessons. When she left school, she took a YTS apprenticeship and studied horse management, and then worked in Epping before moving to Dulverton on Exmoor in 1987. She joined us two years later.

She was conscientious and hard working and won a lot of turnout awards at the races. We never went through anything more than the ups and downs any yard would experience. She was the sort of girl who, when we finished work in the evenings in the summer, would come and play with my boys, Daniel and Hadden, helping them ride their ponies. She was very much part of our family.

I can't remember meeting Stephen because we had grown up together. He was our neighbour on a farm next door to Hawson half a mile away. He lived in a lovely old house, which had lots of staircases, and we'd play there during our summer holidays. It was a great farm. We'd go to the pony shows together, ride up to the village to buy sweets and Mrs Webber always cooked a good Sunday tea.

Through secondary school, we started to drift apart because he was a year older than me, although we would walk home together sometimes, and throughout our time at school we never had an ugly moment. When we left, we carried on our friendship. Stephen was always the first person to come over and help if we had a problem with the cows, he'd help feed up, make hay and did a bit of contract work for us. We had many great days together, drifting ponies off the moor.

Jessie had been working for us for about a year and Stephen had taken quite a fancy to her. He once asked: "Who's the new girl working for you?" He'd help around the yard, hoping to see her, and I kept out of it and left them to naturally drift together.

We believe they had a very short relationship but I don't think they went out together more than half a dozen times, so they were never really an item. And anyway, Jessie wasn't really interested in having a steady boyfriend.

But Stephen started to get obsessive and very protective towards her. Her car would need new tyres, so he'd pick it up and then return it that night with a new set and wouldn't accept any payment for it. He'd buy her TVs, videos and other presents, but all along Jessie was trying to reject his friendship. It was a scenario that went on for about two years.

Before Stephen met Jessie, he'd been admitted to a hospital in Plymouth because he was having trouble with blackouts. He wasn't the type of person to hold a grudge and he never lost his temper, which is the hardest thing to understand about the murder, but he did used to suffer from fits.

Although he never lost his cool, he would have one of these fits if he couldn't get a girlfriend when he was a teenager, and if someone was trying to be a bit cold towards him and turn him away, the same thing would happen.

The doctors never found out what was wrong with him, but I could always tell when an attack was going to come on. More often than not, it was if he was getting stressed over a girl of whom he was fond. I think he found it hard to accept rejection.

Jessie started to go out with one of the local darts team players and that's when things came to a head. It was a Friday and Derek's day off. I was doing his horses for him, so Jessie came round to help and the conversation came round to Stephen. She'd obviously been having some quite heavy problems with him and he'd frightened her a few times.

He was there when she went out to feed at 6am, and on one occasion he'd got quite violent with her after stopping her in her car having chased her home from

Buckfastleigh. She said: "I'm worried. I think I might have to leave because I'm having too many problems with Stephen."

I said: "If you've got a problem Jessie don't treat it lightly."

I knew he'd have trouble with being rejected and her words were beginning to bother me. At the back of my mind I couldn't help thinking that he was capable of losing it with a woman, and I had a niggling feeling that Jessie could be in danger. I said: "Jessie don't mess about. If you think it's getting heavy and there could be a problem, I'll come to the police with you and report what's going on."

By now I was worried because I knew how stressed he could become. It was a Friday and we think Jessie went to play darts in Buckfastleigh. She came home and, unusually, went into the house and asked dad if he would walk her to her caravan where she lived behind the stables.

Dad was worried, so he went to get his torch and told mum about Jessie's concerns over Stephen. Mum said: "Jessie don't be silly. You stay in the house tonight and use the spare room."

Jessie replied: "I'll be okay once I get inside the caravan. I'll have my dog with me so I'll be fine." Jessie was strong willed and you couldn't get her to change her mind, so dad did as she wished and walked her over. I've always wondered how that must play on his mind. At that stage we had no idea how heavy Stephen had become with Jessie and we didn't know until it came out in court.

Jessie always fed the horses first thing in the morning

and when Derek got in at 6.30am, he thought it was odd that no one had fed them. His first thoughts were that perhaps Jessie was ill. There was another younger girl working for us, also called Jessie, and he asked her to find her.

"Why me?" she asked.

"Because you're a girl and it's a girl's bedroom," said Derek.

So Jessie went round the corner and seconds later an ear-piercing scream filled the yard as she ran back. Derek ran to the caravan, saw what had happened, ran back to the house and phoned the police; shouting to mum there had been a murder.

Mum rushed to the caravan, thinking she may be able to help Jessie, and then all hell broke loose. We all knew straight away that it was Stephen who had murdered Jessie. The police arrived. Nobody was allowed to come or go, we weren't even allowed to take water around for the horses until forensics had been in and done their work.

It was claimed in court that the attack was planned. That night, Jessie had been out to a pub with a man called James Pearce, whom she had been seeing for a couple of weeks. Webber admitted the killing in his second police interview. He said he wanted to "get his own back" for the way Jessie had treated him, claiming she had made him "look small".

"I know I had the bar in my hand but that was to frighten her. The plan was not to hit her," Stephen told the police. But he went on to say: "I hit her and hit her . . . I hit her so much I was out of puff."

Jessie had woken up after he had smashed the

window and got into the caravan, and asked what he was doing there. Stephen replied: "I am here to teach you a lesson," adding that he hit her "in temper". In a pre-meditated action, he had taken dad's bar out of his workshop and used it to beat Jessie to a pulp.

After killing Jessie, Stephen drove home, got out of his bloodstained clothing and drove to a friend's house where he had a bath, then dumped the weapon and soiled clothes. He went back to a woman's house in Buckfastleigh and she actually had Jessie's watch in her bedroom.

*

Stephen was picked up driving his car into Buckfastleigh about four hours after the body was found. However, the police nearly had to release him because they could find no evidence.

I was racking my brains thinking where Stephen would have put his clothes and the murder weapon. It could have been anywhere in the wilderness. He'd washed and scrubbed up so well that there was no forensic evidence relating to the murder anywhere – not even under his fingernails. I wondered whether he had used a river but that would not have got rid of the blood.

Then it dawned on me. One of his main jobs was as a relief milkman at a dairy farm – the perfect place to scrub himself down was the dairy with its concrete, hot water and disinfectants. I told the police I believed they would find the evidence where he had been working. At the same time, the police had spoken to some officers who had been patrolling Buckfastleigh following a spate of early morning disturbances from youths. One of them had seen Stephen walking down the street and had passed a couple of comments. He contacted the police in charge of the murder. Stephen had told them he'd been in bed. When they confronted him with the officer's eyewitness account; Stephen broke down and admitted everything.

Stephen was given a life sentence for what the judge called "a terrible act of revenge" at Exeter Crown Court on 18 November 1996. His motive for taking that young person's life was the oldest one in the world – 'if I cannot have her no-one else can'.

Young Jessie, the lass who found her, was really affected, poor kid. You carry those sorts of scars and memories forever. We felt dirty and Hawson changed instantly. The place where I grew up had lost its innocence. Terry Saunders, from Torquay, is a very good friend of mine and he sent his friends up to get rid of the caravan and to clean the place up.

Daniel had nightmares for a long time and he would cry himself to sleep. It was awful. Jessie used to teach him little songs and take him for rides on his pony. She'd given us a load of daffodil bulbs as a present and we all planted them and they started to grow the following spring. We found Daniel sat amongst them crying.

It really makes me squirm when you see those do-gooders on TV trying to rehabilitate murderers. Sixteen years later I could probably talk to Stephen again, but at the time I felt so angry that he could be that selfish. He couldn't sort his own life out so he took someone else's. Taking a life because of jealousy and selfishness is unbelievable. The ricochet was horrendous. It's a small community and the feeling was terrible. Just going to the pub was difficult because some people sympathised with him and thought Jessie deserved it.

We do worry about when he gets out. Do we stay here or do we move? How will we cope with seeing him around? When he comes out, the nightmares will start again for us and a lot of other people. The thing that really shocks me is the value the justice system places on a life. Jessie's life was worth just 12 years because with good behaviour, Stephen will be out in six years' time.

It's a huge part of our history. We all grew up together and we were friends. If I could turn back the clock and relive one moment, I wish I could, because by talking to Stephen I may have been able to help him with his problems. I was leaving the yard with mum to go racing and we were a bit late. It was the time of year when Stephen was trimming the hedges. He pulled into a lay-by, got out of his tractor and walked towards us as we drove by. "Everything alright?" I shouted. He said "yes" but he looked very upset and it was as if he wanted to say something.

"Sorry I've got to keep going, I'm late," I said. That look haunts me now more than anything else. I was his friend and I didn't have time to talk to him. It was the week leading up to the murder. It was all churning over in his head quite heavily, I suspect. If I had stopped and spoken to him, maybe history would be different.

CHAPTER 17

On The Winning Train

The Jockey Club had been pushing me to take over our training licence because they knew dad wasn't very well. They'd pushed me to turn professional, now they were pushing me to take out the licence. I knew the onus was now on me as a trainer, and a whole new chapter of my life was about to start.

On 1 March 2002, my training career began. Four days later, I jumped my final hurdle on Bohill Lad in a handicap at Exeter. All the way up the home straight I thought: "Shall I, I shan't I. Should this be my last ride as a jockey as he is my first winner as a trainer?" It was all perfect. He jumped so well. He was a thrilling ride and one to really enjoy. He went from fifth to first over one hurdle up the back straight. I came over the finishing line and thought: "This is it."

I looked across and said to Richard Johnson: "That's it, let's call it quits." For a moment he had a very blank stare. He later wrote in the *Racing Post:* "We'll all be keen to ride for him, as he's always been recognised as a good judge and, with the experience he gained working for his father, I'm sure he'll make the grade as a trainer." He had more faith in me than I did at the time.

I had spent a long time thinking about retirement, but it was a snap decision. It was the end of an era and life had to change. I had no idea how big a wrench leaving the weighing room would be. Although I always knew the day would come when I actually did chuck my hat and whip into the crowd, it was very emotional and I found it hard to hold back after 30 years in the saddle.

It's something you know you will never do again. Being a jockey isn't a job – it's a passion. The boys in the weighing room are like an extended family. You ride with each other, day in day out, and you get to know each other's moods. The big wins, the cock-ups, the losses, all come back into the weighing room and you either console or congratulate each other.

For a few days, I questioned whether I had given up too soon, my retirement had left such a big hole. I told Nikki to put my racing bag in the loft because I didn't want to see it again, and the sauna was filled up with kids' toys. Life had been comfortable as it was for ten years and I was scared. It felt like I was standing over a precipice.

*

I retired 18 months earlier than I had intended and, when I stopped, I realised I hadn't quite completed 30 years. I was six days short. But it was close enough. I'd ridden the winners of more than 500 races. I'd gone from sellers at Taunton to Grand Nationals at Aintree and back to sellers at Taunton. I didn't miss the riding – I'd worn it out – but I did miss the camaraderie.

I was touched when I read Ian Balding's letter in the *Racing Post*. He said: "Jimmy is the most superb horseman and best rider of a novice our family have ever known. What's more, he's a thoroughly nice guy and everyone I know adores him.

"He's ridden a lot of my better jumpers and the highlight of my association with him has to be his victory on Crystal Spirit in the SunAlliance Novices' at Cheltenham."

However, you can't live your life in the past and I'm in a very fortunate position. I have inherited some very supportive owners, and a training set up that I have been part of for 20 years. It has it all. I have a great team of staff. Derek has been head lad for more than ten years; Liz Vince has worked for us longer than that.

Some of the owners, like Paul Tylor, Jack Joseph, Norman Lake and Janet McCormack, have been with us a long time. I've made some friends for life and, although I've never been any good at remembering Christmases and birthdays, I do enjoy helping people if they are in trouble, like Paul who, not long ago, presented me with a problem I was determined to solve. It involved his sheepdog.

Paul has a very laid-back attitude and two words sum him up – "shit happens". He takes everything in his stride and he's a real gentleman. He has put up with me for nearly 30 years, since I first rode a horse for him called Mena Lodge in 1976. Until the day I retired, I rode a winner for him every season.

A familiar face in the Westcountry, both as a steward

and a breeder of good racehorses and eventers, Paul has been a friend and mentor to me. He also has plenty of land filled with an equal amount of horses, and it's from there that many of Hawson Court's animals come. The trouble is, he leaves them to roam free on the Cornish hilltops until they are four-year-olds and then it's our job to round them up and break them in, and they've never even worn headcollars.

It's the only aspect of racing upon which our opinions differ – I prefer to start my horses when they're two-year-olds but, other than that, we have a good system going. Between us, we've been breeding our own horses for several years.

He has about 15 broodmares and I have six, which I run as a herd with a barn for shelter in the winter. We'll break all the youngsters and progress them along and if one runs well in a bumper, we can introduce a new owner and we'll make some money and have a nice horse to train. If it finishes last, hopefully we've made a nice horse that can do something else, like event or hack.

Five years ago, I spotted Paul was in a bit of trouble. I'd been down working with the horses on his farm and he had a lovely old New Zealand Hunterway dog called Lion. A lot of people wouldn't have seen a dog like Lion because over here they are quite rare, but in New Zealand they are used for working sheep in the high country because they bark. But like everything, it was time for Lion to go to heaven, so that was the end of him.

Paul went to Wales and gave quite a lot of money for a trained collie. But, the trouble is, he didn't come with a manual, and he was probably trained in Welsh, so from the word go they didn't get on. There would be 300 sheep heading in the wrong direction, Paul would blow a fuse and the dog would bolt for home.

He decided to buy another dog because he thought, if one would come, the other would go, and, between them, they ought to be able to round up a flock of sheep, if he trained the pair together.

He was walking with the pair, coupled together with a chain, down the road near his farm and there was a dear old lady walking along. One dog went one side, the other went the other and down she went. That was the final straw.

I'd heard that things weren't going too well for Paul and his dogs, and it was playing on my mind. Mr Lewis, our hay and straw merchant, was at the farm delivering and he asked if I knew of anybody who wanted a puppy.

I asked: "Would it make a good sheepdog?"

Mr Lewis replied: "There's no reason why not, although we've never worked the mother, but he's a Border collie so he ought to be able to."

"Yes, I'd like one," I said.

So he brought down two or three puppies, and we picked them over and chose one, which we called Lewis.

*

Nikki is really into her gun-dogs and trains them to a good standard, so she took on the basic 'sit, stay, come, go' training and taught him like a gun dog. Meanwhile, I took him round with me, getting him used to all the different sights and sounds. When he got to about eight months old, I thought I'd better tell Paul what my plan was, to make sure he'd didn't go and get another dog.

I said: "This is your dog but you can't have him until we've trained him and we've got one problem – I haven't got a clue how you train a sheepdog, so you had better tell me everything you want this dog to learn, and I will try and teach it to him." So he brought me books and videos and told me it was 'cum bye' for left, 'away' for right, and left us to it.

George Welch, a great friend of mine who's a farmer as well as a Jockey Club steward, played a big part and lent me some sheep. I said: "Don't bring valuable ones!" In our lunch hour, Nikki and I would go out and work the sheep, with me holding the book in one hand, shouting out these instructions.

It went pear shaped a few times because the dog was very confused, but we got to the stage where he was virtually at puppy dog trial standard. He would go left, right, go down, bring sheep towards me, split two off, bring them back, take them across the field, and bring them back to the gate.

When George was lambing, we took him over and put him in the lambing shed and he was fine with them. We gave ourselves a big pat on the back and proudly took our dog down to Cornwall when he was 14 months old, and Paul has never had any trouble with his sheep. Given the fact the dog would patiently wait by my side, whilst I thumbed through the manual looking for the next command to teach him, it was his intelligence more than our training that practically enabled him to read the book for himself. He really was a clever dog. When we parted company, Daniel went with him and stayed with him for a few days because he was very attached to him and Paul's been working him ever since. He was a lovely, strong-looking dog and they tell me the collies at the lower end of Cornwall are now a much better breed.

Paul is one of those people you want to ring when you've had a bad day – your perfect 'phone a friend'. He normally says the right thing at the right time and if he doesn't, he still manages to make you feel better.

*

All the owners are comfortable with the arrangement at Hawson Court, but Holybrook is my home and I will move the horses here. When they are just outside your door you can hear if anything is wrong and you live more amongst them. I'm very competitive. I've now got a challenge and I've got to move forward.

I would like an indoor ride, because either the British weather is getting wetter or I'm getting softer, and I can't stand the long wet days. With new ideas and plenty of room to expand, I know I can train horses and succeed.

It only took me three runners to get on the winners' board. Whatever happens now, as I embark on the next phase of my life, I hope that I can give others some of the same chances and emotion as I've had the opportunity to experience myself – not least that win on Little Polveir. Training is great. A fool will lose tomorrow, looking back at yesterday. I had a brilliant yesterday and I'm really looking forward to tomorrow.

APPENDIX

PRINCIPAL RACES WON

1972
3 March DOCTOR FRED (A. Fuller), Maiden, East
Cornwall Hunt Point-to-Point, Lemalla

1973
26 December LOVE SET (Arthur Souch) Amateur
Riders' Novices Hurdle, Wolverhampton – my first
ride under Rules

1974
19 February MOPSEY (R. G. Frost) Motorway
Selling Hurdle, Taunton – first winner under Rules

1981
21 May DEVON SPIRIT (Mrs D. Pook) Westcountry
TV Hunter Chase Championship, Newton Abbot

1987
17 October COMBERMERE (R. G. Frost) Riverdale
Novices' Hurdle, Kempton
28 October COMBERMERE (R. G. Frost) Binfield
Juvenile Novices' Hurdle, Ascot
THE BAKEWELL BOY (R. G. Frost) EBF
Novices' Hurdle Qualifier, Ascot
26 November COMBERMERE (R. G. Frost)
Northern Junior Hurdle, Haydock
1988
17 November BORACEVA (G. B. Balding) Daventry
Novices' Chase, Towcester
2 December MORLEY STREET (G. B. Balding)

PSG National Hunt Novices' Hurdle, Sandown
31 December MORLEY STREET (G. B. Balding)
Ramsbury Hurdle, Newbury.

1989

2 January THE BAKEWELL BOY (R. G. Frost)
David Garrett Memorial Novices' Chase, Devon and
Exeter.

3 January BORACEVA (G. B. Balding) Fairmile
Novices' Handicap Chase, Sandown

19 January THE BAKEWELL BOY (R. G. Frost)
Wolborough Novices' Chase, Newton Abbot

4 February THE BAKEWELL BOY (R. G. Frost)
Scilly Isles Novices' Chase, Sandown

8 February MORLEY STREET (G. B. Balding) AF
Budge Novices' Hurdle, Ascot

27 February BORACEVA (G. B. Balding) Rutland
Water Novices' Chase, Leicester

8 April MORLEY STREET (G .B. Balding) Mumm
Prize Novices' Hurdle, Aintree
LITTLE POLVEIR (G. B. Balding) Seagram
Aintree Grand National Chase Handicap

9 December MORLEY STREET (G. B. Balding)
Mercury Communications Hurdle For Sport of
Kings Challenge, Cheltenham

16 December FOREST SUN (G. B. Balding) HSS
Hire Shops Hurdle, Ascot

29 December FOREST SUN (G. B. Balding)
Challow Hurdle, Newbury

1990

6 January FOREST SUN (G. B. Balding) Baring
Securities Tolworth Hurdle, Sandown

11 January COMBERMERE (R. G. Frost) David
Garrett Memorial Novices' Chase, Devon and
Exeter

23 February FOREST SUN (G. B. Balding) EBF

Novices' Hurdle Qualifier, Kempton.

24 February COMBERMERE (R. G. Frost)
Galloway Braes Novices' Chase, Kempton.

6 March BORACEVA (G. B. Balding) Crudwell Cup,
A Handicap Chase, Warwick.

13 March FOREST SUN (G. B. Balding) Waterford
Crystal Supreme Novices' Hurdle, Cheltenham.

17 March COMBERMERE (R. G. Frost) Tony
Preston Memorial Novices Chase, Chepstow.

7 April MORLEY STREET (G. B. Balding)
Sandeman Aintree Hurdle, Aintree.

20 October MORLEY STREET (G. B. Balding)
Breeders' Cup Chase, Belmont Park, USA.

30 October BORACEVA (G. B. Balding) Derek
Wigan Memorial Chase, Fontwell.

16 November MORLEY STREET (G. B. Balding)
Racecall Ascot Hurdle Grade 2, Ascot.

23 November CRYSTAL SPIRIT (I. A. Balding)
Freshman Novices' Hurdle, Newbury.

1 December BORACEVA (G. B. Balding) Lasmo
Rehearsal Chase Limited Handicap Grade 2,
Chepstow.

3 December MORLEY STREET (G. B. Balding)
Fred Rimell Memorial Novices' Chase, Worcester.

26 December COMBERMERE (R. G. Frost)
Shearings Handicap Hurdle, Kempton

1991

11 January CRYSTAL SPIRIT (I. A. Balding) Silver
Doctor Novices' Hurdle, Ascot.

26 January CRYSTAL SPIRIT (I. A. Balding)
Bishop Cleeve Hurdle Grade 1, Cheltenham.

21 February COOL GROUND (J. Akehurst) Jim
Ford Challenge Cup Chase, Wincanton.

1 March MORLEY STREET (G. B. Balding)
Berkshire Hurdle Grade 2, Newbury.

12 March MORLEY STREET (G. B. Balding)

Smurfit Champion Hurdle Grade 1, Cheltenham.

13 March CRYSTAL SPIRIT (I. A. Balding)
Sun Alliance Novices' Hurdle, Cheltenham.

6 April MORLEY STREET (G. B. Balding)
Sandeman Aintree Hurdle Grade I, Aintree.

12 October MORLEY STREET (G. B. Balding)
Breeders' Cup Chase, Fair Hill, USA.

15 November MORLEY STREET (G. B. Balding)
Racecall Ascot Hurdle Grade 2, Ascot.

26 November COMBERMERE (R. G. Frost) Woolea
Retail of Street and Wells Handicap Chase, Devon
and Exeter.

30 December BORACEVA (G. B. Balding) Derek
Wigan Memorial Chase, Fontwell.

31 December SPINNING (I. A. Balding) Lansdown
Novices' Hurdle, Cheltenham.

1992

7 January COMBERMERE (R. G. Frost) Johnny
Clay Memorial Handicap Chase, Chepstow.

17 January SPINNING (I. A. Balding) Ashford
Novices' Hurdle, Kempton.

5 February COMBERMERE (R. G. Frost)
Charterhouse Mercantile Handicap Chase, Ascot.

22 February FOREST SUN (G. B. Balding)
Rendlesham Hurdle, Grade 2, Kempton.

29 February CRYSTAL SPIRIT (I. A. Balding)
Berkshire Hurdle Grade 2, Newbury.

3 March COMBERMERE (R. G. Frost) Culinaire
Crudwell Cup Handicap Chase, Warwick.

3 April SPINNING (I. A. Balding) Cordon Bleu
Handicap Hurdle, Aintree.

3 May SPINNING (I. A. Balding) Swinton Handicap
Hurdle, Haydock.

1993

26 March TOPSHAM BAY (D. H. Barons) Paul

Croucher Memorial Trophy Handicap Chase, Newbury.

30 October CRYSTAL SPIRIT (I. A. Balding) BonusPrint Novices' Chase, Warwick.

10 November CRYSTAL SPIRIT (I. A. Balding) Hallow'een Novices' Chase, Newbury.

11 December CRYSTAL SPIRIT (I. A. Balding) BonusPrint Novices' Chase, Cheltenham.

1997

9 November COOME HILL (W. W. Dennis) Badger Beer Handicap Chase, Wincanton.

2002

5 March BOHILL LAD (J. D. Frost) Exeter Racecourse Conference Centre Handicap Hurdle, Exeter – a winner on my last ride and my first winner as a trainer.

INDEX

The index is arranged alphabetically except for personal subheadings, which appear in approximate chronological order.